LEGO INDIANA JONES
THE ORIGINAL ADVENTURES
PRIMA OFFICIAL GAME GUIDE
WRITTEN BY
STEPHEN STRATTON

Senior Product Manager: Donato Tica
Editor: Rebecca Chastain
Copyeditor: Sara Wilson
Design and Layout: Calibre Graphix, LLC
Manufacturing: Suzanne Goodwin

ISBN: 978-0-7615-5918-4

Library of Congress Catalog Card Number: 2008920937

Printed in the United States of America

08 09 10 11 GG 10 9 8 7 6 5 4 3 2 1

PRIMA GAMES
An Imprint of Random House, Inc.
3000 Lava Ridge Court, Suite 100
Roseville, CA 95661
www.primagames.com

Stephen Stratton

Stephen Stratton has authored over 40 guides in his seven years with Prima. His personal favorites include *Resident Evil 4: Wii Edition, Mercenaries: Playground of Destruction, Mass Effect,* and pretty much every guide he's written that has either "Mario" or "Zelda" in its title.

Stephen is a lifelong video gamer who attended the Rochester Institute of Technology in Rochester, NY. In addition to his Prima Games guides, he also held a staff position with Computec Media and managed the strategy section of their incite.com video game website.

We want to hear from you! E-mail comments and feedback to sstratton@primagames.com.

P9-BJA-203

CONTENTS

INTRODUCTION

Welcome to LEGO® Indiana Jones™: The Original Adventures!

Thank you for purchasing Prima's Official Game Guide to *LEGO Indiana Jones: The Original Adventures*. We've spared no effort in crafting an easy-to-use guide full of maps and game screens—one that reveals all aspects of Indy's action-packed, blockbuster adventure!

The Saga of Indiana Jones

Raiders of the Lost Ark—1981

Deadly traps. Massive tumbling boulders. *Snakes*. A devious villain and an artifact of unimaginable power. What's not to love about *Raiders of the Lost Ark*, Indy's very first flick? So many memorable moments all rolled into one ground-breaking film.

The Temple of Doom—1984

As if being poisoned by Chinese mobsters wasn't enough, Indy soon ends up falling into the hands of a evil cult bent on world domination in the series' second, high-thrills installment. Awesomely huge and creepy bugs, chilled monkey brains, and white-knuckle mine cart rides stick with us long after this one ends—this author's personal favorite!

The Last Crusade—1989

This brilliantly crafted tale of good versus evil not only taught us the value of listening to our dads and choosing wisely, it also taught us Indy's true name—Henry Jones Jr.! (Apparently they named the dog Indiana … but Indy had a lot of fond memories of that dog.) This is one of the series' most beloved installments and a true masterpiece of the Action/Adventure genre.

How to Use This Book

The information in this guide is presented in four chapters. Here's what you'll find in each one:

Adventurer's Handbook

The next few pages of this guide teach you the basics of sound adventuring. From game mode overviews to adventuresome actions, from vital items to a tour of Barnett College, you'll find this chapter a great resource when first getting your bearings.

Walkthrough

By far the largest chapter of the guide, our walkthrough guides you through every challenge and obstacle Indy faces in his block-based adventure. Every area is covered in each level, with labeled maps taken straight from the pages of Henry Jones's Grail diary. Whether you follow the walkthrough step-by-step or simply reference it whenever you become stuck, you're sure to find it an invaluable resource.

Characters

There's a stunning number of characters for you to unlock in *LEGO Indiana Jones*—more than 80! This section of the guide details almost every character you can play with, including each one's weaponry and special abilities.

Bonus Features

While the Characters chapter and walkthrough reveal many of *LEGO Indiana Jones*'s hidden goodies, we've kept all of the really hush-hush stuff separate in the final pages of the guide. From super-secret characters to bonus stages and quick-reference tables that reveal info on cheat codes, parcels, and achievements, you'll find all of the game's best-kept secrets uncovered in the Bonus Features chapter.

ADVENTURER'S HANDBOOK

Looking for fortune and glory, eh kid? The two go hand in hand, but only the most daring adventurers will ever find them. Do your homework and read this little handbook, where you'll learn all the basics of high-risk adventuring.

Game Modes

There are two game modes in *LEGO Indiana Jones*: Story mode and Free Play. You must play each level in Story mode first; after you beat a level, you're able to revisit it in Free Play mode to explore it more thoroughly.

Story Mode

In Story mode, each level plays out much as it would in the *Indiana Jones* films. You always control Indy and one or more supporting characters— folks who would normally appear during that segment of the movie. For example, you control Indy, Willie, and Short Round during most *Temple of Doom* levels. You're treated to brief and humorous cinematics during Story mode, and you're usually given just enough skills among your characters to get through the stage.

NOTE

Once you've beaten the first *Raiders* level, you're free to play the first levels from *Temple of Doom* and *The Last Crusade*.

Free Play Mode

Free Play mode does away with the cinematics and character limitations. It sets you free in each level, letting you use a variety of characters who might not even belong to the *Indiana Jones* flick you're playing. You choose your main character when starting up Free Play, but that's all; the game automatically scans the characters you've unlocked and picks out a group you'll use—one that sports the best array of skills for the level you're about to play. You may toggle your Free Play character to any member of your group at any time.

Once you've unlocked a few dozen characters in Story mode, you'll likely be able to do whatever you please during Free Play. Spy a goodie or area that you can't seem to reach? It's a safe bet that you need to revisit the level in Free Play to check it out.

Adventurous Actions

Fighting

The life of the dauntless adventurer is filled with great danger and devious double-crossers. To survive, you'll need to keep your wits about you and fight back with everything you've got. Fists are always an option, but everything's a weapon to the cunning explorer. Chairs, bottles, and anything else you can get a hold of are yours for the taking—and tossing!

Weapons

Of course, when the going gets rough, there's nothing better than having a real weapon at your side. Get your hands on one of these babies if you can:

Swords: Great for hacking stuff up, and you can also throw them at distant targets. They're handy for cutting ropes, too.

Spears: A lot like swords, really. Try 'em out!

Crossbows: These only seem primitive until you're shot by one.

Pistols: Now we're talking! Six good shots, six fewer bad guys.

Machine guns: Why fire one bullet at a time when you can squeeze off three at once?

Bazookas: If you can't smash it or shoot it, try blowing it up. Just be careful, kid—you can really hurt yourself with these things.

Breaking Stuff

Beating up bad guys is a big part of adventuring in *LEGO Indiana Jones*, but so is smashing stuff. Punch everything you see to find all sorts of goodies, from loose change to vital items.

Building Stuff

Sometimes punching things won't help you. Sometimes, you need to build stuff to get ahead. If you notice a pile of jiggling LEGO bits lying on the ground, try stacking them to see what you can build.

Boxes of Bits

You might also discover a box full of LEGO bits from time to time. They're pretty common, really. Place the boxes on special green pads to dump out their contents so you can stack those loose bits.

Pushing Stuff

If you can't break it or stack it, you probably need to push it. Checkered floor tiles are a dead giveaway; every adventurer knows you can push stuff along a checkered floor. Look around and see if there are any statues or crates nearby that might need a shove.

Handles

Some objects have orange handles. These are also dead giveaways; push against a handle to grab it, then keep pushing. If nothing happens, try pulling backward and see if you can't yank the handle out. Handles are tricky that way.

Spinners

Lastly, in the "pushing stuff" department, we have spinners. These usually have a big handle with one green side and one red side. Green means go, so push against the green side of the handle to make the spinner, um, spin. Keep spinning that spinner until something cool happens (other than your getting dizzy).

Using the Whip

The best adventurers carry whips, because they know that whips are awesome and multipurpose tools. Use your whip to trip up enemies, or even steal away their weapons. Your whip will also help you get past loads of obstacles: Whenever you spot a glowing wooden pallet on the ground (which every true adventurer knows is called a whip point), stand there and use your whip to do something adventurous, like swinging across a chasm or yanking something useful toward you.

Digging

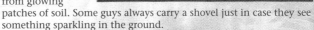

Here's a vital piece of adventuring know-how: Digging for treasure is totally profitable. Find a shovel and you can excavate all sorts of long-lost items and artifacts from glowing patches of soil. Some guys always carry a shovel just in case they see something sparkling in the ground.

Repairing

Machines are always breaking down, you know? It's frustrating, but you can fix broken gizmos pretty easily. Just get your hands on a wrench and you'll be able to fix any hunk of sparking, smoking junk.

Reading Glyphs

At some point, every serious adventurer encounters mysterious hieroglyphics left behind by ancient civilizations. Unfortunately, it seems that people of old really liked leaving their glyphs in the form of puzzles. Find a special little blue book, though, and you'll be able to crack the code and solve these little brain-teasers with ease.

Vital Items
Keys

Keys have a variety of uses. They usually open doors and the like, but sometimes, the turn of a key can cause platforms to align inside a dark chamber, letting you cross the room to steal a golden idol from the depths of a trap-filled temple. Sometimes keys do that, but not often.

One sure thing about keys is that they always fit inside special mechanisms. If you ever find a key just lying around, pick it up and look for a suitable mechanism to stick it in. Then turn the key and see what happens.

Torches

Torches are useful in many situations. Lighting up dark places is a big advantage of the torch, but you probably already figured that. What you may not know is that torches are great for scaring off snakes and bugs. If some creepy crawlers are creepily crawling in your path, reach for a torch and have no fear.

Dynamite

It's a well known fact amongst veteran explorers that silver objects can't be destroyed by normal means. No, the only way to destroy a silver object is to blast it with something explosive, like a bazooka. Unfortunately, bazookas are hard to come by these days, but dynamite makes for a great substitute. Throw some dynamite at something silver and watch it go boom!

Tantalizing Treasures
Studs

Studs are the main currency in *LEGO Indiana Jones*. Fortunately, they're lying all over the place, so it's easy to get rich. Collect every stud you see, and smash every breakable object you encounter to find even more.

Silver studs are common and worth 10 studs.

Gold studs are uncommon and are worth 100 studs.

Blue studs are rare and are worth 1,000 studs.

Purple studs are the rarest of all—each one's worth a whopping 10,000 studs!

TIP

Earn True Adventurer status from each level by collecting enough studs to fill the True Adventurer bar at the top of the screen. See each level's walkthrough to learn how many studs you need to achieve this goal.

Artifact Pieces

Studs are pretty common, but artifact pieces are rare finds. Search high and low for these worthy prizes. There are 10 hidden in each level, and some are far more difficult to claim than others. Collect all 10 artifact pieces from a level to complete the level's artifact. Complete all the artifacts in the game to unlock some really cool bonus stuff!

Parcels

The most precious and rarest prize of all, parcels hold the secrets of true adventuring goodness. Find one parcel in each level, then find the level's postbox and mail the parcel back to Barnett College. Visit the college's mail room afterward and buy the parcels you've discovered to unlock all sorts of cool stuff! See the Bonus Features chapter at the end of this guide for complete details.

Barnett College

We've all got day jobs, right? Although he's really a super-amazing adventurer, Dr. Jones pays the day-to-days as a professor of archeology at Barnett College.

There's lots of cool stuff to check out at the college, so let's have a quick tour.

Main Hall: All of the adventure begins right here! Approach one of the hall's three bulletin boards to view the levels that are available to you across each Indy film. Which adventure will it be this time, Dr. Jones?

Library: All characters you've encountered in Story mode but haven't unlocked can be purchased at the library. Time to brush up on your history! See the Characters chapter for info on each character you can unlock in the game.

Mail Room: Every parcel you find and mail during your adventures ends up at Barnett College's mail room. Spend some studs to buy one and claim a new power! See the Bonus Features chapter for details.

Art Room: Dash through the courtyard to reach the art room, where you can create your own vision of the perfect Free Play adventurer! Parts from every character you've unlocked so far are available for use, including heads, hats, torsos and legs. Custom characters you've made will appear on the bottom row of the Free Play character selection screen (there are 2 custom character slots).

Classroom: We didn't put all of those cheat codes into the Bonus Features chapter for nothing! Check them out and then input the ones you like at the classroom's chalkboard.

Theater: Get yourself a big bucket of buttery popcorn before paying a visit to the theater room, where you can watch all of the Story mode cinematics you've unlocked so far.

Indy's Office: There's something very strange about Dr. Jones's office. Check out the Bonus Features chapter for full disclosure.

Artifact Room: You've worked hard to collect all those artifact pieces. Why not pay a visit to the college's artifact room sometime, where each artifact you've collected is proudly displayed? Real adventurers know it's OK to take pride in your accomplishments!

NOTE

There's more to Barnett College than meets the eye. Flip to the Bonus Features chapter at the end of this book to uncover the college's hidden mysteries!

CHARACTERS

GLOBThere are a whopping 82 characters for you to unlock in *LEGO Indiana Jones*. Here we detail the unique fighting styles, weaponry, and special abilities possessed by every character in the *LEGO Indiana Jones* universe!

Unlocking Characters

Each time you complete a story mode level, you automatically unlock all of the characters you controlled during that stage. For example, you unlock Willie and Short Round after beating the first *Temple of Doom* level. Other characters you encounter during Story mode—enemies and the like—also become unlocked after you beat each stage. However you must visit Barnett College's library to purchase characters you've encountered in Story Mode but didn't get to control.

Character Abilities

Most levels feature special areas and goodies that you can't visit or collect during your first run-through. To fully explore all of the levels, you must revisit them in Free Play mode with a group of characters who possess a wide range of skills and abilities. Put the information in this chapter to good use and unlock characters with lots of special abilities to get the most out of Free Play!

Ability Descriptions

Academic ability: Characters with this ability can solve glyph puzzles.

Enemy disguise ability: These characters look just like the enemy and can fool guards at guard posts, gaining entry to special areas.

Excavate ability: Characters with this ability carry around a shovel at all times. This allows them to paddle about in rafts and dig up buried objects from glimmering soil.

 Explosion ability: These characters can destroy silver LEGO objects with their unlimited supply of explosive weaponry.

Glass-shattering ability: Characters with this ability can break open glass containers and the like.

Repair ability: These characters can fix broken machinery with their trusty wrenches.

Super jump ability: All female characters have this ability and can jump higher than other characters.

Tiny size ability: Children and other small characters have this ability, which enables them to crawl through tiny doors to reach special areas.

Thuggee chant ability: Characters with this ability can perform a special chant at Kali statues, which causes a special change in the environment to occur.

 NOTE

Characters armed with weaponry have unlimited ammo for that weapon. If their weapon is one that can be thrown (such as a sword or spear), the weapon is automatically replaced shortly after they toss it. Handy!

Bandit

Abilities:
Cost to Buy: 15,000
Weaponry: None
Notes: A common outlaw encountered in Cairo.

Bandit Swordsman

Abilities:
Cost to Buy: 25,000
Weaponry: Sword
Notes: A ruffian armed with a curved sword.

Barranca

Abilities: None
Cost to Buy: 18,000
Weaponry: Pistol
Notes: One of Indy's cowardly jungle guides in *Raiders*.

Bazooka Trooper (Crusade)

Abilities:
Cost to Buy: 30,000
Weaponry: Bazooka
Notes: An enemy trooper that's armed with a powerful bazooka.

Bazooka Trooper (Raiders)

Abilities:
Cost to Buy: 30,000
Weaponry: Bazooka
Notes: An enemy trooper that's armed with a powerful bazooka.

Belloq

Abilities:
Cost to Buy: 50,000
Weaponry: None
Notes: Indiana's arch nemesis in *Raiders*.

Belloq (Jungle)

Abilities:
Cost to Buy: 50,000
Weaponry: None
Notes: Indiana's arch nemesis dressed in jungle attire.

Belloq (Robes)

Abilities: None
Cost to Buy: 50,000
Weaponry: None
Notes: Belloq in his ceremonial Ark-opening garb.

Boy Scout

Abilities: None
Cost to Buy: None (unlocked during Story mode)
Weaponry: None
Notes: A young boy scout—one of Young Indy's pals.

British Commander

Abilities: None
Cost to Buy: 30,000
Weaponry: Pistol
Notes: A guest at the Pankot Palace dinner party.

British Officer

Abilities: None
Cost to Buy: 25,000
Weaponry: Pistol
Notes: A guest at the Pankot Palace dinner party.

British Soldier

Abilities: None
Cost to Buy: 18,000
Weaponry: Pistol
Notes: A guest at the Pankot Palace dinner party.

Brody

Abilities:
Cost to Buy: None (unlocked during Story mode)
Weaponry: None
Notes: Indy's longtime friend and colleague.

Captain Katanga

Abilities:
Cost to Buy: 18,000
Weaponry: None
Notes: Captain of the ship Indy boards after recovering the Ark.

Chatter Lal

Abilities:
Cost to Buy: 40,000
Weaponry: None
Notes: Pankot Palace's dignitary and high-ranking cult member.

Chatter Lal (Thuggee)

Abilities:
Cost to Buy: 40,000
Weaponry: None
Notes: Chatter Lal in his ceremonial cultist garb.

Chen

Abilities: None
Cost to Buy: 18,000
Weaponry: Machine gun
Notes: One of Lao Che's right-hand men.

Colonel Dietrich

Abilities:
Cost to Buy: 50,000
Weaponry: Pistol
Notes: High-ranking enemy in *Raiders*.

Colonel Vogel

Abilities:
Cost to Buy: 50,000
Weaponry: Pistol
Notes: High-ranking enemy in *Crusade*.

Dancing Girl

Abilities:
Cost to Buy: 27,500
Weaponry: None
Notes: An attractive female dancer who works at Club Obi-Wan.

Donovan

Abilities:
Cost to Buy: 50,000
Weaponry: None
Notes: Evil antique collector who'll do anything to possess the Holy Grail.

Elsa

Abilities:
Cost to Buy: None (unlocked during Story mode)
Weaponry: None
Notes: Attractive female historian who secretly works for the enemy.

Elsa (Desert)

Abilities:
Cost to Buy: 15,000
Weaponry: None
Notes: Elsa in her desert attire.

Elsa (Officer)

Abilities:
Cost to Buy: 15,000
Weaponry: None
Notes: Elsa in her enemy officer's uniform.

Enemy Boxer

Abilities: None
Cost to Buy: 25,000
Weaponry: None
Notes: A burly enemy boxer who fights Indy at the airfield in Cairo.

Enemy Butler

Abilities: None
Cost to Buy: 15,000
Weaponry: None
Notes: Castle Brunwald's evil butler.

Enemy Guard

Abilities:
Cost to Buy: 18,000
Weaponry: Pistol
Notes: A common enemy soldier.

Enemy Guard (Mountains)

Abilities:
Cost to Buy: 30,000
Weaponry: Pistol
Notes: An enemy soldier encountered in the snowy mountains of Nepal.

Enemy Officer

Abilities: 🧨🎖️🔪

Cost to Buy: 30,000

Weaponry: Hand grenade (potato mashers)

Notes: A high-ranking enemy officer that throws explosives.

Enemy Officer (Desert)

Abilities: 🧨🎖️🔪

Cost to Buy: 30,000

Weaponry: Hand grenade (potato mashers)

Notes: An enemy officer in a desert uniform.

Enemy Pilot

Abilities: None

Cost to Buy: 25,000

Weaponry: Pistol

Notes: An enemy fighter pilot who harasses Indy and his dad in *Crusade*.

Enemy Radio Operator

Abilities: 🎖️

Cost to Buy: 25,000

Weaponry: Pistol

Notes: An enemy communications officer encountered at Castle Brunwald.

Enemy Soldier (Desert)

Abilities: 🎖️

Cost to Buy: 18,000

Weaponry: Pistol

Notes: An enemy soldier in desert uniform.

Fedora

Abilities: None

Cost to Buy: 25,000

Weaponry: Pistol

Notes: An adventuresome man that Indy encounters in his youth and comes to idolize.

First Mate

Abilities: 🔧

Cost to Buy: 12,500

Weaponry: None

Notes: Captain Katanga's first mate. He carries a wrench just like his captain.

Grail Knight

Abilities: 🔪

Cost to Buy: 100,000

Weaponry: Sword

Notes: An ancient warrior who guards the Holy Grail.

Henry Jones

Abilities: 📖

Cost to Buy: None (unlocked during Story mode)

Weaponry: None

Notes: Indy's studious father and the foremost authority on the Holy Grail.

Hovitos Tribesman

Abilities: 🔪

Cost to Buy: 18,000

Weaponry: Spear

Notes: A South American tribal warrior.

Indiana Jones

Abilities: None

Cost to Buy: None (unlocked during Story mode)

Weaponry: Whip

Notes: The star of the show in his traditional adventuring garb.

Indiana Jones (Army Disguise)

Abilities: 🎖️

Cost to Buy: None (unlocked during Story mode)

Weaponry: Whip

Notes: Indy in his *Raiders* army disguise.

Indiana Jones (Desert Disguise)

Abilities: None

Cost to Buy: 27,500

Weaponry: Whip

Notes: Indy in his desert outfit, worn when tracking down the Ark in Cairo.

Indiana Jones (Desert)

Abilities: None

Cost to Buy: None (unlocked during Story mode)

Weaponry: Whip

Notes: Indy in his desert attire.

Indiana Jones (Dinner Suit)

Abilities: None

Cost to Buy: None (unlocked during Story mode)

Weaponry: Whip

Notes: Indy in his Club Obi-Wan dinner jacket.

Indiana Jones (Kali)

Abilities: None

Cost to Buy: None (unlocked during Story mode)

Weaponry: Whip

Notes: Indy in his cultist garb.

Indiana Jones (Officer)

Abilities: None

Cost to Buy: 18,500

Weaponry: Whip

Notes: Indy in his enemy officer's uniform, worn when he retrieved the Grail diary from Elsa.

Indiana Jones (Professor)

Abilities: None

Cost to Buy: None (unlocked during Story mode)

Weaponry: Whip

Notes: Indy's casual Barnett College attire.

Jock

Abilities:

Cost to Buy: None (unlocked during Story mode)

Weaponry: None

Notes: Indy's pilot friend in *Raiders*.

Jungle Guide

Abilities: None

Cost to Buy: 18,000

Weaponry: Pistol

Notes: One of Indy's cowardly guides from the beginning of *Raiders*.

Kao Kan

Abilities: None

Cost to Buy: 25,000

Weaponry: Machine gun

Notes: One of Lao Che's right-hand men.

Kazim

Abilities: None

Cost to Buy: 30,000

Weaponry: Pistol

Notes: A member of the mysterious brotherhood dedicated to keeping the Holy Grail safe and undiscovered.

Kazim (Desert)

Abilities: None

Cost to Buy: 30,000

Weaponry: Pistol

Notes: Kazim in his desert ambush attire.

Lao Che

Abilities: None

Cost to Buy: 19,000

Weaponry: Machine gun

Notes: An evil Chinese mobster who attempts to poison Indy at Club Obi-Wan.

Maharajah

Abilities: 🗡️🔦

Cost to Buy: 40,000

Weaponry: None

Notes: The boy-prince of Pankot Palace and high-ranking cult member.

Major Toht

Abilities: None

Cost to Buy: 50,000

Weaponry: Pistol

Notes: A high-ranking enemy who harasses Indy and Marion at Café Raven.

Marion

Abilities: 📇

Cost to Buy: None (unlocked during Story mode)

Weaponry: None

Notes: A beautiful young woman who owns a small pub in Nepal.

Marion (Cairo)

Abilities: 📇

Cost to Buy: None (unlocked during Story mode)

Weaponry: None

Notes: Marion in her desert attire.

Marion (Evening Dress)

Abilities: 📇

Cost to Buy: None (unlocked during Story mode)

Weaponry: None

Notes: Marion in a lovely evening dress given to her by Belloq.

Marion (Nightgown)

Abilities: 📇

Cost to Buy: None (unlocked during Story mode)

Weaponry: None

Notes: Marion in a silk night gown given to her by Captain Katanga.

Masked Bandit

Abilities: ⚔️

Cost to Buy: 18,000

Weaponry: Sword

Notes: A mask-wearing bandit armed with a curved sword.

Mola Ram

Abilities: ✋

Cost to Buy: 50,000

Weaponry: None

Notes: The wicked cult leader of Pankot Palace who seeks to rule the world.

Monkey Man

Abilities: None

Cost to Buy: 27,500

Weaponry: None

Notes: A one-eyed man in Cairo who owns a trained monkey.

Pankot Assassin

Abilities: ⚔️

Cost to Buy: 25,000

Weaponry: Sword

Notes: A dangerous assassin that attacks Indy at Pankot Palace.

Pankot Guard

Abilities: ⚔️

Cost to Buy: 18,000

Weaponry: Spear

Notes: One of Pankot Palace's royal guards.

Sallah (Desert)

Abilities:

Cost to Buy: None (unlocked during Story mode)

Weaponry: None

Notes: Indy's good friend who assists him on many adventures.

Sallah (Fez)

Abilities:

Cost to Buy: None (unlocked during Story mode)

Weaponry: None

Notes: Sallah in his favorite hat.

Satipo

Abilities:

Cost to Buy: None (unlocked during Story mode)

Weaponry: None

Notes: A shifty jungle guide who assists Indy at first, then betrays him.

Sherpa Brawler

Abilities: None

Cost to Buy: 18,000

Weaponry: Pistol

Notes: One of many hard-nosed ruffians that attack Indy and Marion in Nepal.

Sherpa Gunner

Abilities: None

Cost to Buy: 25,000

Weaponry: Machine gun

Notes: A dangerous man with a powerful machine gun.

Short Round

Abilities:

Cost to Buy: None (unlocked during Story mode)

Weaponry: None

Notes: Indy's pint-size pal who follows Dr. Jones on many adventures.

Slave Child

Abilities:

Cost to Buy: 3,000

Weaponry: None

Notes: One of the many children kidnapped by Pankot Palace's cult and forced to work in the mines.

Thuggee

Abilities:

Cost to Buy: 18,000

Weaponry: Sword

Notes: A low-level cultist armed with a curved sword.

Thuggee Acolyte

Abilities:

Cost to Buy: 30,000

Weaponry: None

Notes: A high-ranking cultist.

Thuggee Slave Driver

Abilities:

Cost to Buy: 18,000

Weaponry: None

Notes: A burly cultist who forces the slave children to work in the mines.

Village Dignitary

Abilities: None

Cost to Buy: 15,000

Weaponry: None

Notes: A wise man whose people are being tormented by Pankot Palace's evil cult.

Village Elder

Abilities: None

Cost to Buy: 15,000

Weaponry: None

Notes: An old wise man who pleads with Indy to help save his village's children.

Willie

Abilities:

Cost to Buy: None (unlocked during Story mode)

Weaponry: None

Notes: A beautiful singer Indy meets at Club Obi-Wan. She can shatter glass with her powerful singing voice.

Willie (Ceremony)

Abilities:

Cost to Buy: None (unlocked during Story mode)

Weaponry: None

Notes: Willie in the garb the cultists dress her in.

Willie (Dinner Suit)

Abilities:

Cost to Buy: 15,000

Weaponry: None

Notes: Willie in a formal dinner suit.

Willie (Evening Dress)

Abilities:

Cost to Buy: 15,000

Weaponry: None

Notes: Willie in a beautiful evening dress.

Willie (Pajamas)

Abilities:

Cost to Buy: None (unlocked during Story mode)

Weaponry: None

Notes: Willie in her Pankot Palace pajamas.

Wu Han

Abilities: None

Cost to Buy: 20,000

Weaponry: Machine gun

Notes: Indy's good friend who disguises himself as one of Club Obi-Wan's waiters.

Young Indy

Abilities: None

Cost to Buy: None (unlocked during Story mode)

Weaponry: Whip

Notes: Indy as a boy.

THE LOST TEMPLE

Raiders of the Lost Ark

South America, 1936

The adventure begins with a crew of explorers delving deep into the heart of a dense, steamy jungle. It is rumored that an artifact of great value rests within a long-forgotten temple somewhere nearby. His nose buried in an ancient map, our fearless hero deftly avoids tumbling into pitfalls as he leads his team onward in search of fortune and glory. Sadly, many of his companions aren't so lucky!

STAGE COLLECTIBLES

Item	Area	Notes	Got It?
📦₁	1	Behind tree near the start	☐
📦₂	1	On low ledge (dig up 3 golden statues to reveal)	☐
📦₃	2	Behind brush near steps	☐
📦₄	2	Inside waterfall cave	☐
📦₅	3	Far-right nook of lower trail	☐
📦₆	4	Inside side room (explosion ability required)	☐
📦₇	5	Activate Kali statue; solve glyph puzzle along lower trail (academic ability required)	☐
📦₈	6	Inside side room (explosion ability required)	☐
📦₉	7	Inside statue mouth (shoot eyes)	☐
📦₁₀	7	In brush to the left	☐
📦	5	Along lower trail (activate Kali statue; thuggee chant and glass-shattering abilities required)	☐

True Adventurer stud requirement: 30,000 studs

Helpful Free Play Skills:

- Academic ability
- Explosion ability
- Glass-shattering ability
- Thuggee chant ability

STORY MODE CHARACTERS

Indiana Jones   **Satipo**   **Jock**

Area 1: Jungle Path

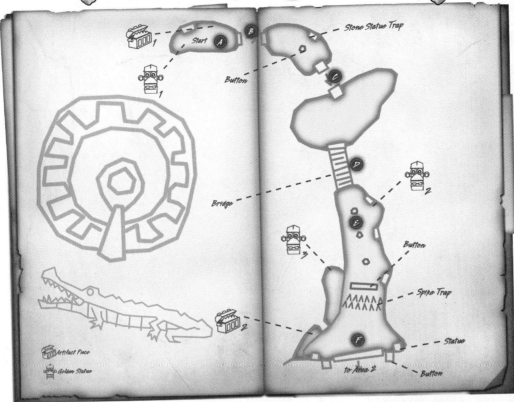

Welcome to the Jungle

Indiana Jones and his remaining companion, Satipo, are on a small, overgrown ledge. Familiarize yourself with Indy's moves as you run about, pressing the Attack button to smash apart the many nearby plants, weeds, and stone statues for studs.

NOTE

Studs are currency in *LEGO Indiana Jones*. They're used to purchase new characters and the like at Barnett College. Collect lots of studs to earn True Adventurer status from each level! See the Adventurer's Handbook chapter for more on studs.

After thoroughly exploring the starting ledge, use the hanging vine to swing cross this gap.

TIP

Find extra studs by climbing vines before you leap from them. Always search high and low for studs!

Stand on the nearby wooden pallet and use Indy's whip to swing across this next gap. Satipo can't cross so easily; have Indy punch a wooden box after he lands to free a vine so that Satipo can follow.

NOTE

Wooden pallets like this are known as "whip points." These are spots where Indy can use his whip for special purposes. Keep this ability in mind!

Have Satipo dig up an odd LEGO object from the nearby sparkling ground, then use the object to build a bridge across this pit.

Artifact Piece 1

Objects that can be collected or carried are commonly highlighted by a blue arrow. If an object is meant to be placed somewhere special (like this LEGO object), a white arrow points out that special location while you carry the object.

Search behind the large tree near the level's start to find your first artifact piece.

The final golden statue is buried at the far end of the low ledge near the gate. Destroy some weeds to find it.

Artifact Piece 2

Avoid the many stone statue traps along this path as you dash onward. (Punch all the statue heads to turn them into silver stud dispensers if you like.)

Find and excavate three golden statues in this area to reveal a hidden artifact piece. The first golden statue is buried right near the start—you can't miss it.

The artifact piece now appears on the low ledge near the gate. Be sure to collect your hard-earned prize!

Opening the Gate

NOTE

All artifact pieces are shown on the maps. Some artifact pieces can be obtained only during Free Play. Collect all ten artifact pieces from a level to complete its artifact! See the Adventurer's Handbook chapter for details.

As Satipo, dig up a large statue head that's buried in the ground here. Carry and place the head atop the stone pillar to the left of the gate, then push against the pillar to reveal a button. Shove the other pillar near the gate, then step on both buttons to open the way forward.

The second golden statue is buried beneath a stone statue beyond the bridge. Smash the statue to reveal the dig spot.

Area 2: Waterfall

Raft Action

Spikes and Spiders

Build a raft out of the jiggling pile of LEGO blocks near the water.

Satipo's shovel acts as a paddle for the raft. Pilot the raft as Satipo so you can safely cross the croc-infested pond.

Pummel the spiders that drop in to attack you here, and beware the spikes that jut up from the ground near the sealed door. Hang from the pair of vines near the door to open it. (Each character must hang from one of the vines.)

TIP

Before leaving the raft, paddle toward the foreground and collect studs along the water's edge.

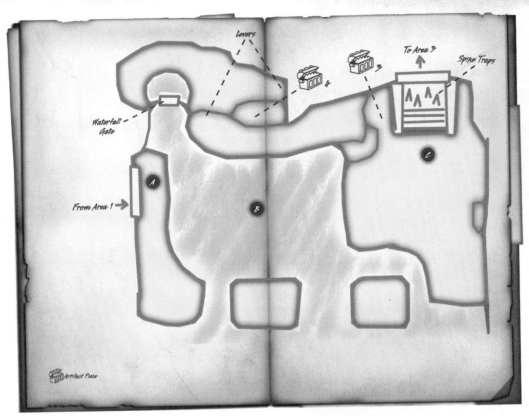

CAUTION

Beware: More spiders will drop in and attack from time to time!

Artifact Piece 3

Search the thick growth to the left of the steps to discover this artifact piece

Artifact Piece 4

Leap up the stacked rocks to the left of the steps to reach a narrow background ledge. Pull the lever at the ledge's far end to lower the gate in front of the waterfall.

Drop into the pond and swim into the waterfall to discover a secret cave!

Yank the lever inside the waterfall cave to make a brick pop out of the wall. Use the brick as a stepping stone to help you reach the artifact piece on the ledge above.

Area 3: Pitfall Path

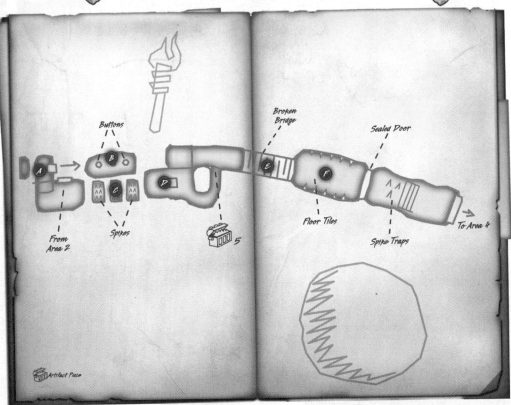

Take the High Road

As Indy, jump and climb to the ledge above the entryway. Use Indy's whip at the whip point there to reach the high ledge to the right.

Place the crate you find up here on the middle button, then position Indy atop the button to the left. Wait for Satipo to begin navigating the lower trail, then move Indy onto the far-right button so Satipo can proceed.

Drop down and cross the lower trail as Indy after Satipo disables the spike trap.

Build a Ladder, Cross a Bridge

Use Indy's whip at the whip point here to yank a nearby lever and obtain some LEGO bits. Build a ladder out of the bits and climb up to the trail above.

Dash across this bridge as fast as you can before its boards give out.

Tricky Tiles

Open the sealed door ahead by solving the floor tile puzzle here. Four of the floor tiles are slightly depressed; quickly leap from one sunken floor tile to the next to make each one rise up in turn. Raise all four sunken tiles without delay to open the giant sealed door ahead.

CAUTION

Stepping on any of the nonde-pressed floor tiles causes arrows to fly out from the skulls along the walls. Jump with care!

⚜ Artifact Piece 5 ⚜

Carefully navigate a curvy ledge to discover this artifact piece tucked away in a hidden nook.

Area 4: Idol Chamber

Secret Key

At last, Indy and Satipo have reached the heart of the temple. Jump and hang from the nearby vine to open a trapdoor in the ceiling. Out falls a key. Insert the key into the mechanism on the wall, then turn it to rotate the room's platforms.

South American Idol

Cross the platforms after you align them and approach the golden idol in the room's center. Indy steals the idol, and in so doing, triggers an ancient trap. The entire temple starts shaking as it begins to collapse!

Carefully leap across the now-rotating platforms, escaping the chamber through the background doorway.

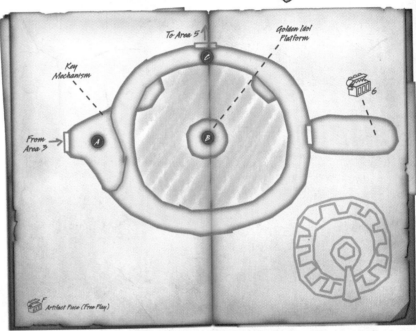

Free Play Goodie

⚜ Artifact Piece 6 ⚜

After snatching the golden idol, toggle your Free Play character to one with the explosion ability and blow up the silver bars on the chamber's right wall. This opens up a secret passage!

Jump across the rotating platforms and head into the passage you've opened to collect an artifact piece from a small side room.

Area 5: Hazard Trail

Let's Get Outta Here!

Jump and swing on a hanging vine to cross this first wide chasm. Climb the vine if you'd like to nab a few valuable studs.

Take cover in this pathway's background nooks to avoid being crushed by the giant stone heads that periodically fall from above.

Leap out and swing across the vine that dangles above this gap to reach the far end of the trail.

Both Indy and Satipo must hang from the two overhead vines here to raise a platform behind them. A stone head then falls, bounces off the platform, and rolls down the trail, smashing through the wooden boards ahead and opening up an escape route.

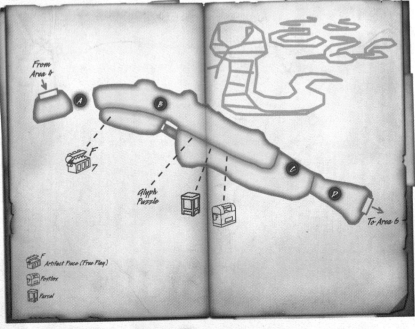

From Area 4

Glyph Puzzle

To Area 6

F Artifact Piece (Free Play)

Postbox

Parcel

Free Play Goodies

Parcel

This level's Parcel is found in this area. Use a character that has the Thuggee chant ability to activate the Kali statue in this area during Free Play mode. This removes the spikes from the lower pathway so you may explore down below. (See the Characters chapter for complete details on all characters, how to unlock them, and the special abilities they possess.)

The postbox and Parcel await discovery in the lower trail. Use a character with the ability to shatter glass to get at the Parcel,

then carry the brick to the postbox and mail it back to Barnett College. (Check the Bonus Features chapter to get the skinny on Parcels.)

Artifact Piece 7

Use a character with the academic ability to solve the glyph puzzle at the lower trail's far end. This causes a bridge to extend across the gap to the left so you may access a secret side room.

Dash across the bridge and enter the side room to find loads of studs and an artifact piece. Nice haul!

Area 6: Boulder Chase

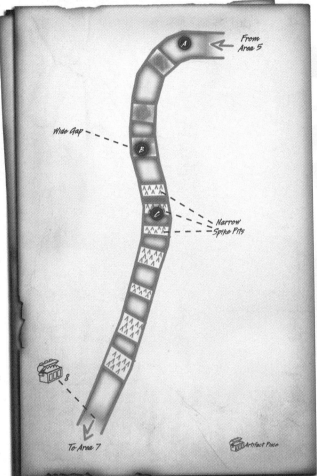

Artifact Piece 8

Reach the end of the boulder run and you can nab an artifact piece from the tunnel's far end. However, if the boulder hits you, you're unable to claim this artifact piece. Complete the level and then try again!

NOTE

The manner in which Indy and Satipo exit the tunnel varies depending on whether they manage to outrun the boulder or are flattened by it.

Run for Your Life!

Just when Indy and Satipo think they've escaped certain doom, a massive boulder begins tumbling toward them. Waste no time in dashing toward the foreground, fleeing the rolling boulder.

TIP

Don't go out of your way to smash objects or collect studs—just focus on dodging pitfalls and keeping ahead of that boulder.

Dodge the first two pits with normal jumps, but press the Jump button twice to execute a diving leap across this wider third gap.

Slow down a bit and make short, careful hops to clear this trio of narrow spike pits. Then make a mad dash toward daylight, leaping every pit that follows with diving double-jumps.

Area 7: Escape Route

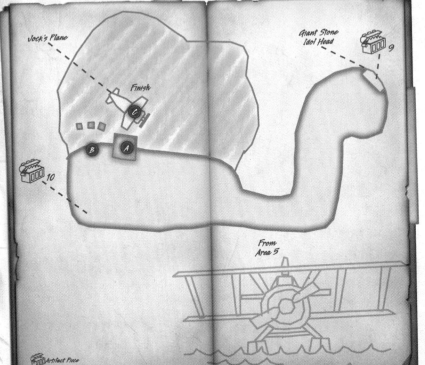

Artifact Piece 9

Before fixing the plane and escaping, explore the jungle's right side to discover a huge stone idol head. Use the spears and crossbows dropped by defeated Hovitos tribesmen to strike the statue's eyes. (Indy will target the eyes when facing them with a weapon in hand.)

Strive to collect hearts dropped by defeated Hovitos to keep Indy in good health and studs in your bankroll. Whenever Indy dies, hurry to reclaim the studs he drops.

If Only You Spoke Hovitos

You must repair Jock's plane to escape the jungle. Find a box of LEGO bits on the shore near the plane and drop them on the green pad here.

Stand on the whip point here and use Indy's whip to snag another box of LEGO bits from the water near Jock's plane. Drop this second box of bits on the green pad as well, then stack the bits to assemble the plane's propeller.

After assembling the propeller, take control of Jock and jump up the nearby boxes to reach the top of the plane. Use Jock's wrench to fix the propeller by holding the Use button to initiate repairs. Indy and Jock make their escape the moment the plane is fixed. Level complete!

Put out both of the stone idol's eyes to open its jaws so you may retrieve the artifact piece from within its mouth.

Artifact Piece 10

This artifact piece is a gimme—explore the far-left half of this area to find it hidden in the brush.

INTO THE MOUNTAINS

Having heard of Indiana's incredible knowledge in the field of all things shiny and old, a few government bigwigs task our intrepid adventurer with the heavy job of locating the long-lost Ark of the Covenant—a legendary and divine artifact of unimaginable power. Indy knows he'll need the help of an old and once-dear friend to find the Ark—a beautiful young woman named Marion. Wasting little time, Indiana immediately sets off for the frigid hills of Nepal, where Marion runs a little-known pub called Café Raven.

STAGE COLLECTIBLES

Item	Area	Notes	Got It?
1	1	In fireplace (hang from ropes to reveal)	☐
2	1	Behind bar (pull balcony lever to access)	☐
3	2	Dig up snowmobile, smash barricades (excavate ability required)	☐
4	2	Inside a shack (blow up silver boards; explosion ability required)	☐
5	2	Find and build 3 snowmen	☐
6	3	On high ledge (tiny size ability required)	☐
7	3	On low ledge (glass-shattering ability required)	☐
8	4	Near exit steps (solve glyph puzzle to reveal; academic ability required)	☐
9	5	Beyond closed gates (use lift and start generator)	☐
10	5	In brazier (use torch from previous area to light and reveal)	☐
	2	Left by Santa (enter house near Café Raven to trigger; enemy disguise ability required)	☐

True Adventurer stud requirement: 35,000 studs

Helpful Free Play Skills:

Academic ability

Enemy disguise

Excavate ability

Explosion ability

Glass-shattering ability

Tiny size ability

STORY MODE CHARACTERS

Indiana Jones   **Marion**

Area 1: Café Raven

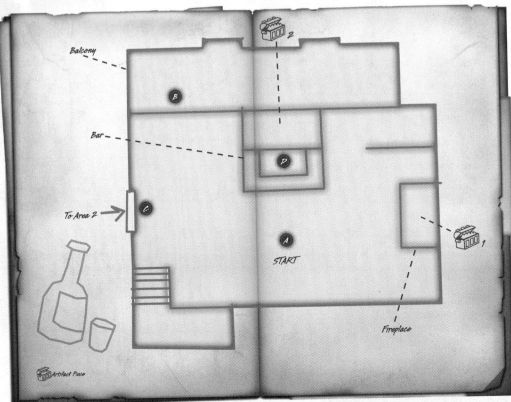

Balcony

B

Bar

D

To Area 2 → C

A
START

1

Fireplace

Artifact Piece

Bar Hopping

All's quiet inside Marion's pub—but not for long! Spend some time smashing stuff inside Café Raven for fun and profit.

TIP

Build objects out of jiggling LEGO blocks you discover inside the café, then smash those objects for even more studs!

Female characters can jump much higher than male characters in *LEGO Indiana Jones*. Use Marion's superior jumps to reach the pub's background balcony, where a key is found.

When you've finished ransacking Marion's pub, use the key you found on the balcony to unbar the front door.

Unwelcome Visitors

Marion and Indy receive unwelcome guests just as they're about to leave—Major Toht and several Sherpa brawlers storm into the bar. Time for a bar fight!

Showdown: Major Toht

Major Toht's goons are just a distraction: Toht is the real target here. Notice that his portrait is displayed at the top of the screen, with four hearts lined up below. This means you must hit Toht four times with fists or foreign objects to defeat him and escape the café.

Defeat Sherpa brawlers for hearts and help keep Indy's health up to snuff.

Toht is quick to run away, so try tossing chairs and bottles at him from afar instead of punching him up close. Wait until the blue targeting arrows appear around Major Toht before throwing an object at him.

After defeating Major Toht, you're faced with a dangerous Sherpa gunner. Toss chairs and bottles at the Sherpa gunner from range until you best him as well.

Snag chairs and bottles from the foreground to keep out of the Sherpa gunner's firing range.

Major Toht reappears after you best the Sherpa gunner, and this time, he's packing a pistol. Be quick to collect the machine gun that the Sherpa gunner dropped after being defeated, then open fire on Toht to cut him down in short order. Toht and his henchmen then retreat. Marion and Indy flee the café as it becomes consumed by flames.

Artifact Piece 1

Jump up and grab the low rope that hangs near the fireplace to tip the heating cauldron and reveal an artifact piece. Switch to Marion, then jump and grab the higher rope near the fireplace to lower the cage so you may collect your prize.

Artifact Piece 2

Use Marion to reach the bar's upper balcony. Smash some crates at the balcony's far end to reveal a lever. Stack the nearby LEGO bits to reassemble the lever, then pull it. This sends some barrels crashing through the wooden boards behind the bar.

With the boards out of your way, search behind the bar to find a hidden artifact piece. Score!

Area 2: Snowy Street

Nepal at Night

Lash armed enemies with Indy's whip to steal their weaponry!

Don't let your guard down: More Sherpa brawlers rush and attack you just outside Marion's flaming café. Many of these goons are armed with pistols, so be quick to dispatch each wave that appears.

Map on next page!

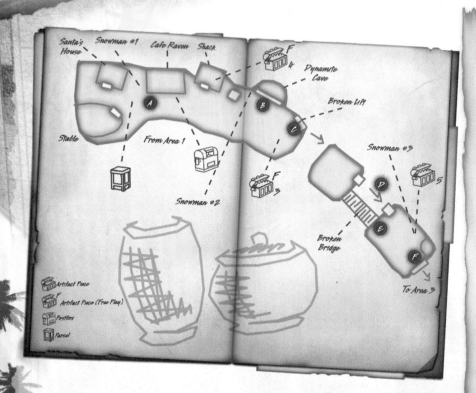

Free Play Goodies (Continued)

Artifact Piece 3

Bring a character who carries a shovel to this area in Free Play mode and dig up parts of a snowmobile from the sparkling snow just outside Café Raven. Stack the parts afterward to assemble the snowmobile, then hop on.

Smash through five barricades that now appear along the snowy street to make an artifact piece appear nearby. Cool!

Artifact Piece 4

During Free Play mode, use a character that can blow up stuff to destroy the silver boards that block the door of the shack to the right of Café Raven. Enter the shack and nab an artifact piece from within.

Free Play Goodies

Parcel

Visit this area in Free Play mode and use a character with the enemy disguise ability to fool the guard at the window of the house to the left of Café Raven. The guard opens the door and lets you in.

Hey look—it's Santa Claus! The unmistakable figure comes bounding down the chimney and dashes out of the house, leaving a trail of studs. Hurry and follow him outside!

Find a box of LEGO bits inside the house and use it to build a rope hook near the fireplace. Use Indy's whip to yank on the hook from the ground.

Santa's nowhere in sight, but he's left a fantastic prize behind: a parcel! Deposit the parcel into the nearby postbox (which now stands in front of Café Raven), to send it back to Barnett College.

Fun with TNT

Silver objects, such as the boards that block entry to the small cave here, can only be destroyed by explosives. Snatch a torch from one of the nearby sconces and light the dynamite, then touch the dynamite to light its fuse. Run away before it goes boom, then some jiggling LEGO bits inside the cave.

Build a pallet out of the LEGO bits inside the cave and place the pallet at the broken lift here. Use the wrench you find in the nearby box to fix the lift's engine, then ride up to reach the overhead handrail. Shimmy across to the gap to the right.

Use Indy's whip to swing across this next gap. Marion can't cross just yet.

Stack the jiggling LEGO bits you discover here to assemble a bridge, then shove the bridge to the left so that Marion can cross the gap.

As Marion, leap onto the nearby ledge and shove the barrel of dynamite onto the ground below. Stack the dynamite, then backtrack to retrieve a torch. Light the dynamite's fuse to blast the silver boards that block your progress to the next area.

✦ Artifact Piece 5 ✦

Find and build three snowmen in this area to reveal a hidden artifact piece. The first snowman is right near Café Raven—destroy the logs and stack the LEGO bits that spill out to build it.

The second snowman is inside the dynamite cave—smash a barrel to find its bits, then stack those bits to build it.

The third and final snowman is just across the bridge. Use a torch to light the dynamite, then stack the LEGO bits that are left behind.

After building all three snowmen, an artifact piece appears close by. Thanks, Frosty!

Area 3: Mountain Pass

Runnin' Round the Mountain

Use Indy's whip to cross this area's first pit, then stack the pile of LEGO bits you discover on the opposite side to create a handrail for Marion.

Free Play Goodie

✦ Artifact Piece 6 ✦

During Free Play mode, use a small character, such as Short Round, to reach a hidden artifact piece. Smash away the ice on the first stretch of path to reveal a tiny door, then send your bite-size pal crawling through.

You pop out of a matching door on a high ledge. Toggle your Free Play character back to Indy, then whip-swing over to a nearby ledge. There you find an artifact piece!

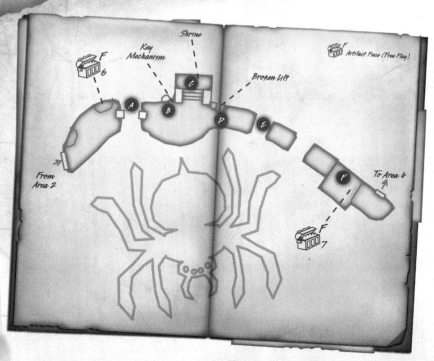

Carry the pallet over to the nearby broken lift and set it down on the green pad. Use the wrench you recently found to fix the lift's engine so you can ride up to a higher stretch of trail.

Beware of Falling Ice

Thin ice shatters as you navigate the trail, exposing dangerous pits. Make long, double-jump leaps across each gap you encounter.

Statue Bashing

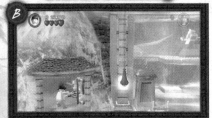

Use Marion's superior jumping skill to reach a key mechanism in a high nook here. Turn the key to open a massive pair of doors in the cliff ahead, revealing an odd shrine.

Smash the two columns near the shrine's steps to reveal a wrench and some handrail bits. Assemble the handrail, then use it to reach the ledge above.

Shove the large statue off the ledge, then drop off in pursuit. Quickly assemble a pallet out of the remains of the statue you shoved.

CAUTION

A mob of Sherpa gunners soon swarms you. Beat them up as fast as you can!

Use the handrails to cross this final gap, then dash through the doorway beyond.

Free Play Goodie
🧱🔧 Artifact Piece 7 🔧🧱

Revisit this area in Free Play mode and use a character that can shatter glass to free an artifact piece that's trapped within some ice on a low ledge.

Area 4: Cavern Chamber

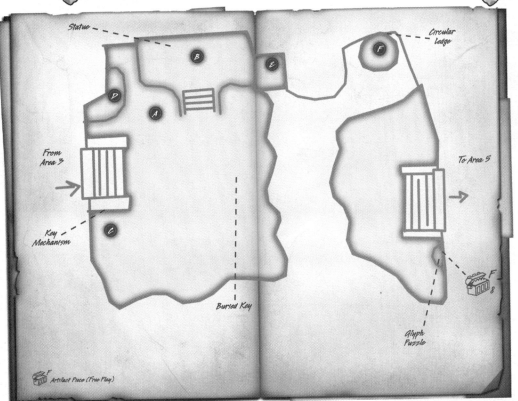

Statue

B

E

Circular Ledge

F

D

A

From Area 3

To Area 5

Key Mechanism

C

Buried Key

Glyph Puzzle

F 8

F Artifact Piece (Free Play)

Crossing the Cavern

A

Smash the two odd objects that stand at either side of the background steps in this giant cavern. A shovel pops out of the left object; use it to dig up a key from a shimmering patch of ground to the right.

B

Shove the massive statue here to the left as far as it will go.

C

Use the key you found to activate a mechanism near the entry stairs. This causes an overhead rope to lower. Jump up and climb the rope to reach the ledges and handrails above the entry.

D

Leap from the final handrail and land atop the statue you shoved earlier. Take control of your other character, then shove the statue all the way to the right. The statue's "passenger" then leaps off, landing on a remote ledge.

E

Switch characters again and build a rope out of the jiggling LEGO bits atop the ledge. The other character climbs the rope and joins you. When both characters are standing on this ledge, a circular ledge pops out of a wall to the right.

F

Jump and shimmy across the handrails to reach this circular ledge, then leap for a nearby rope. Swing across the gap to reach the doorway at the cavern's far-right side.

Free Play Goodie

Artifact Piece 8

Use a character with the academic ability to solve the glyph puzzle near the cavern chamber's exit. This causes a few tiny ledges to pop out of the rock face above, one of which sports an artifact piece!

Area 5: Truck Depot

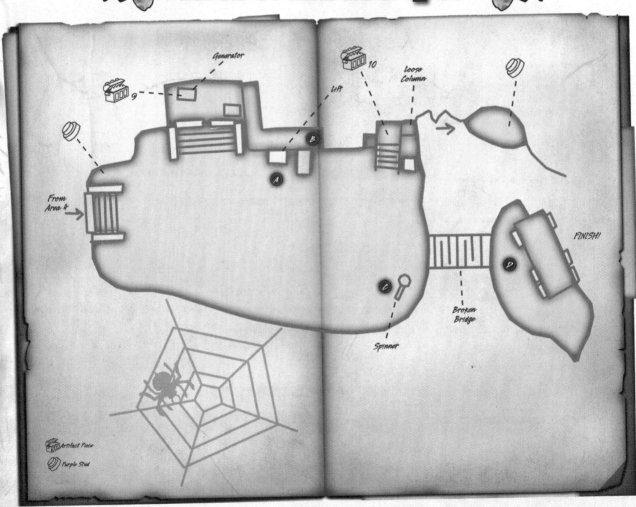

Rooftop Bazooka

Hop onto the nearby llama and steer the animal onto the large pressure plate to the right. This causes the adjacent wooden platform to rise like an elevator, allowing you to reach the rooftop above.

Collect the bazooka from the rooftop's far end, then drop down to the street.

Blast the silver box here, then stack the jiggling bits to build a spinner. Push against the spinner to repair the nearby bridge. Defeat the enemy soldiers who rush you, then cross the bridge.

CAUTION

Act fast—more soldiers will emerge from the truck bed if you dally!

Use your bazooka to blow up the shiny silver truck beyond the bridge. This clears your escape route out of Nepal. Level complete!

TIP

Before leaving the area, use Indy's whip at the whip point to topple a large column. The column now serves as a bridge; cross it to reach a valuable purple stud on the far ledge!

Artifact Piece 9

Before destroying the truck and fleeing the area, find a wrench inside a barrel near the closed gates. Ride the nearby lift to reach the rooftop, then drop off to the left to land in the area behind the gates.

Use your wrench to fix the broken engine beyond the gates. This causes the gates to swing open.

Smash some objects near the area's entry steps to discover an odd LEGO block. Carry this block through the now-open gates and place it onto the generator.

The generator starts up, runs for a moment, then explodes into an artifact piece. How about that?

Artifact Piece 10

Backtrack to the previous cavern and retrieve a torch from near the stairs. Carry the torch back to this area and use it to light the large brazier atop the steps.

Once lit, the brazier bursts into an artifact piece. Jump up and claim your prize!

MOTORCYCLE ESCAPE

Tracking Down the Ark

The hunt for the Ark has led Indiana to Cairo, a massive and beautiful city built upon the desert sands of Egypt. Unfortunately, Indy isn't the only one searching for the Ark here—the enemy is everywhere, eager to put a stop to our hero's meddling efforts. Egypt's capital will soon tremble under the might of an epic clash between the forces of good and evil!

STAGE COLLECTIBLES

Item	Area	Notes	Got It?
1	2	On monkey ledge (glass-shattering ability required)	☐
2	2	Inside guard barracks (enemy disguise ability required)	☐
3	2	On high ledge in alley (smash mud/flowers; build ladder)	☐
4	3	In side room (enemy disguise ability required)	☐
5	3	Inside large canister (tiny size ability required)	☐
6	3	Blow up metal boards; shove object from rooftop (explosion ability required)	☐
7	4	On roof behind background wall (build ladder to reach)	☐
8	5	On high rooftop (blow up fan and rebuild to reach; explosion ability required)	☐
9	5	On low ledge near area start (drop off roof)	☐
10	6	On high ledge (tiny size and explosion abilities required)	☐
	6	Inside cantina (solve glyph puzzle to access; academic ability required)	☐

True Adventurer stud requirement:
55,000 studs

Helpful Free Play Skills:

Academic ability

Enemy disguise ability

Explosion ability

 Glass-shattering ability

 Tiny size ability

STORY MODE CHARACTERS

Indiana Jones
(Desert)

Marion
(Cairo)

Area 1: Outer Street

Monkey Business

Indy and Marion—in full desert attire—are standing on a small street on the outskirts of Cairo. Take a banana from a nearby crate and toss it at the monkey on the high ledge to win its favor. The monkey then tosses a wrench down to Indy.

Don't attack the robed civilians in the street. They're harmless at first, but they'll throw down if you take a swing!

Use the wrench to fix the broken lift here. Ride up to the landing above and dash through the doorway to reach the next area.

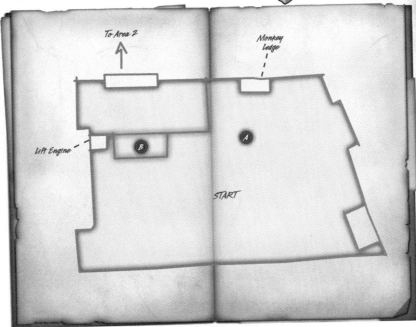

Area 2: Market

Just Browsing

The market area is much larger with lots to see and do. Smash apart the metal railing here, then stack the jiggling LEGO bits that spill out to form a ladder on the wall.

Watch out, Indy: Black-hooded guards (called masked bandits) patrol the market, and they'll attack you on sight!

Snatch a banana from a nearby cart and hurl it up at the monkey, who now sits on a ledge above the ladder. The monkey tosses down a shovel; use it to dig up the handle of the nearby lever, then reattach the lever's handle and pull it to extend the ladder you built.

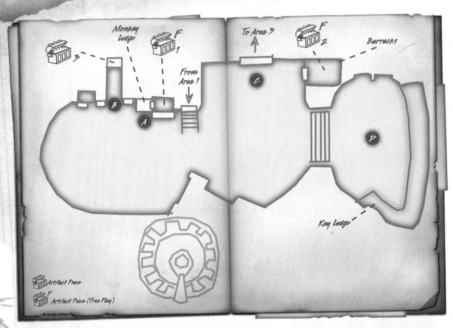

Climb the ladder and then bounce along the cart awnings to the left, heading for the key here.

Insert the key into one of the two mechanisms near sealed gate here. One more key to find!

Free Play Goodies
Artifact Piece 1

Use a character with the glass-shattering ability to smash through

Free Play Goodies (continued)

the window on the monkey ledge so you may claim the artifact piece from the small room beyond.

Artifact Piece 2

During Free Play mode, use a character with the enemy disguise ability to fool the guard at the window near the gate. The guard then grants you access to the barracks.

Pull the lever within the barracks four times and defeat each enemy soldier that storms in to attack you. The fourth time you pull the lever, an artifact piece appears instead of a guard!

The Second Key

Push the rolling cart here to the left as far as it will go. Next, take control of Marion and jump on top of the awning in the corner. Leap from the awning and land atop the cart you've just pushed.

Jump from the cart and grab a dangling rope to raise a platform. Leap from the platform to reach a tall ledge where the second key sits. Return to the gate and use this second key to open it.

Artifact Piece 3

Punch the piles of mud (dung?) on the ground inside this narrow alley to transform each pile into beautiful flowers. Next, destroy the flowers to reveal a jiggling pile of ladder pieces. Assemble the ladder, then climb up and claim the artifact piece from the ledge above.

Area 3: Plaza

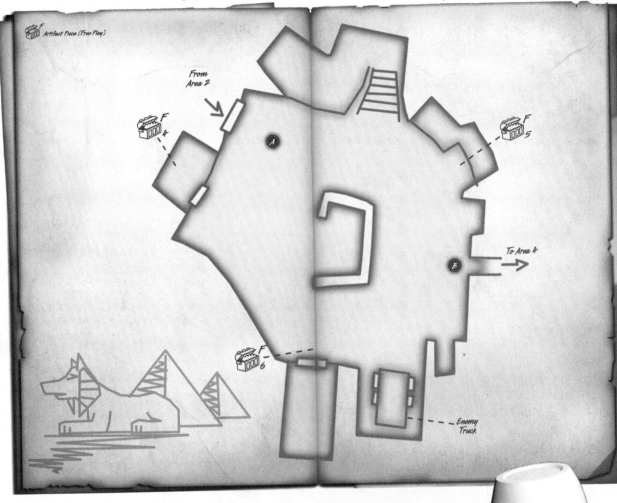

Artifact Piece (Free Play)

From Area 2

F 4

F 5

A

B

To Area 4

F 6

Enemy Truck

Carts and Camels

Indy and Marion are met by soldiers riding camels in this wide-open area. Punch those camels to defeat these enemies before they stomp you.

CAUTION

Keep alert. More soldiers will regularly appear from the truck that's parked in the alley!

Stack the jiggling LEGO bits near the large cart here to form a handle. Push against the handle, then pull away to drag the cart backward. Dash into the alley beyond to reach the next area.

Free Play Goodies

 Artifact Piece 4

During Free Play mode, switch to a character that sports the enemy disguise ability so you may fool the guard at the window along the plaza's left wall. The guard opens the door to a secret room.

Smash the various objects within the room to reveal some jiggling LEGO bits, then stack these bits to form a TV set. An artifact piece appears after you complete the entire object.

 Artifact Piece 5

Use a small character to crawl through the tiny door along the plaza's outer wall. This takes you to the balcony above.

Once atop the balcony, toggle your Free Play character back to Indy and use his whip to yank open the giant canister hanging to the right. Out spills an artifact piece!

 Artifact Piece 6

Use a character that owns the explosion ability to blow up the silver boards near the soldiers' truck. Dash through the doorway and climb the stairs beyond.

Place the box of LEGO bits you find on the rooftop on the nearby green pad, then stack the bits to form a heavy object. Shove the object to the left and off the roof. The object smashes on the ground, revealing an artifact piece!

Area 4: Back Alley Stairs

Going Up!

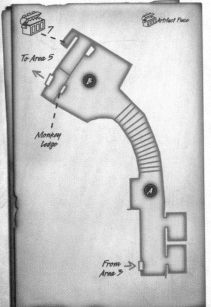

As you dash through the alley, a gang of masked bandits ambushes you here. More hostiles attack you as you climb the steps ahead. Show 'em who's boss!

TIP

Steal a masked bandit's sword to make fighting these brutes a little easier.

Use Indy's whip to tug the railing off the monkey ledge atop the steps. This causes the monkey to fall, bringing it down to your level.

Snag a banana from the nearby cart and toss it to the grounded monkey to receive some dynamite in exchange. Quickly hurl the dynamite at the shiny, silver barrel that's holding a ladder in place against the wall. This destroys the barrel, causing the ladder to drop down. Climb up to the roof and continue toward the next area.

⚜ Artifact Piece 7 ⚜

Stack the pile of jiggling LEGO bits at the top of the stairs to create a ladder up the wall. Climb the ladder, then use the handrail and ledge to the right reach the roof.

There's an artifact piece up here that's very well hidden. Carefully creep along the roof's right edge, then turn left and slip behind the background wall. Aha! Gotcha!

Area 5: Rooftop Maze

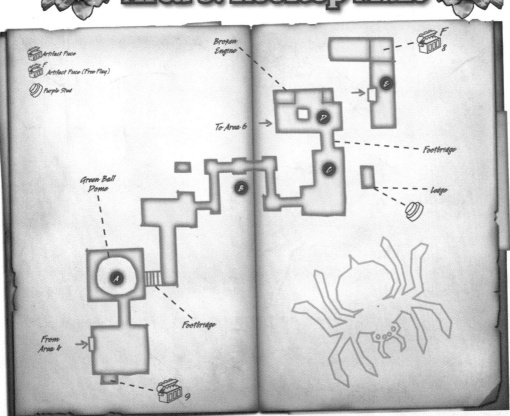

Cairo's Heights

A Push against the green panel here to reveal some steps on the nearby dome. Run up the steps and shove the green ball to the right. The ball bounces down the steps and hits a board on the adjacent rooftop, knocking it over and creating a footbridge.

B Use care when crossing the wooden planks around here. The boards are rotten and collapse when you cross! If you start to fall, try grabbing onto the lower handrails to save yourself.

C Take a banana from a crate here and toss it at the monkey on the nearby ledge to receive a key. Use the key on the nearby mechanism to extend a bridge to the next rooftop.

TIP

Use Marion's awesome jumping ability to reach the distant ledge to the right, where a valuable purple stud is found. It's well worth the effort because it's worth 10,000 studs!

Toss another banana to the monkey here to receive a wrench. Use the wrench to fix the nearby engine, causing an object to fall from the awning above. Place the object on the nearby green pad.

Use Indy's whip to cross over to the rooftop to the right. Punch the wooden wall there to shatter it into LEGO bits, then stack those

bits to form a bridge leading back to the previous roof. Pick up the nearby object and carry it across the bridge, setting it down on the same green pad as before.

Stack the now-jiggling LEGO bits on the green pad to form a giant lever. Jump and grab onto the lever's handrail to pry open a trapdoor in the roof. Drop through the trapdoor to reach the next area.

Free Play Goodie
Artifact Piece 8

Use a character with the explosion ability to destroy the shiny metal fan on the far-right rooftop. Next, stack the bits that remain to build a different sort of fan that blows upward. Jump into the fan's current to float up, then land atop the nearby roof to claim an artifact piece.

Artifact Piece 9

Run toward the foreground and drop off the very first rooftop in this area, grabbing onto a low handrail. Drop to the tiny ledge below, where you discover a hidden artifact piece.

Area 6: Truck Depot

Beware of Boom-Sticks

This final area is crawling with enemy soldiers, including officers that wear dark clothing. Take advantage of dropped weaponry and be quick to defeat each group of hostiles.

CAUTION

Enemy officers toss explosive grenadelike objects called "potato mashers." Keep away from these dangerous boom-sticks!

Defeat an enemy officer in this area and pick up the special hat he leaves behind. While wearing this hat, your character is disguised as the enemy! Knock on the window near the locked gate here, and the guard will think you're one of them. The guard then opens the nearby door for you.

Stack the jiggling LEGO blocks near the broken truck here to reassemble its engine. Smash a nearby barrel to find a wrench, then use the wrench to repair the truck. Hop into the driver's seat and smash right through the locked gate.

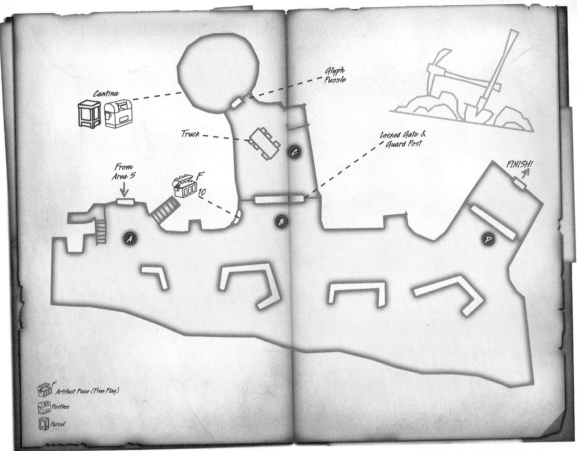

Cantina

Glyph
Puzzle

Truck

Locked Gate &
Guard Post

From
Area 5

F
10

FINISH!

C

B

A

D

F
Artifact Piece (Free Play)

Postbox

Parcel

Free Play Goodies

⬛🧍 Artifact Piece 10 🧍⬛

Use a character with the explosion ability to blow up the silver cage surrounding the tiny door to the left of the guard booth. Switch to a tiny character afterward and crawl through the door.

You pop out of a matching tiny door high above. Collect the artifact piece up here before dropping back down to the ground.

⬛⬛ Parcel ⬛⬛

Solve the glyph puzzle on the background wall behind the truck to open the nearby door. Head inside to visit a familiar-looking cantina.

Stack the jiggling bits near the cantina's dance floor to build a pair of speakers, then pull off some fancy footwork to light up all of the floor's spaces. Drop The parcel then appears in the middle of the dance floor; drop it in the nearby postbox.

Truckin'

Have fun with the truck, which is heavy enough to smash through many of the silver objects in this area. When you're ready to get a move on, smash right through the giant metal gate at the far end of town. Exit the truck and head through the narrow doorway—on a motorcycle if you prefer. Level complete!

THE WELL OF SOULS

Well, Well, Well

Having successfully infiltrated the enemy's excavation site—a massive operation headed by none other than Indy's arch nemesis, Belloq—Indiana Jones and his good friend, Sallah, finally find the clue that pinpoints the exact location of the Ark's long-lost resting place: a giant underground tomb called the Well of Souls. Belloq's cronies are digging in the wrong place, but Dr. Jones knows it won't be long before they discover this sacred chamber. The Ark must be recovered with all speed!

STAGE COLLECTIBLES

Item	Area	Notes	Got It?
1	1	Behind giant Anubis statue (use Sallah)	☐
2	2	Lower bridge and open secret nook to the right to find (tiny size and explosion abilities required)	☐
3	2	Solve light puzzle in secret chamber after lowering bridge	☐
4	3	Destroy silver statue (explosion ability required)	☐
5	3	Smash weak bricks in left wall to discover	☐
6	6	Drop to low ledge to reach	☐
7	6	Cross the rotating handrails to reach	☐
8	7	Use Marion to close 3 snake shutters and reveal	☐
9	8	In spike-filled chamber (academic ability required)	☐
10	9	In high nook (whip-swing across pit and climb rope)	☐
	9	In secret area off high nook with 10th artifact piece	☐

True Adventurer stud requirement:
57,000 studs

Helpful Free Play Skills:

Academic ability

Explosion ability

Tiny size ability

STORY MODE CHARACTERS

Indiana Jones Sallah (Desert) Marion (Evening Dress)

Area 1: Snake Pit

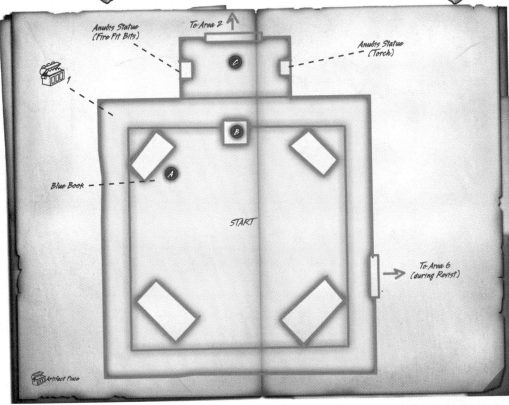

Anubis Statue
(Fire Pit Bits)

To Area 2

Anubis Statue
(Torch)

C

1

B

Blue Book

A

START

To Area 6
(during Revisit)

Artifact Piece

Why'd It Have to Be Snakes?

A

Smash apart the clay vases here to discover a small, blue book. Collect the book for future use.

CAUTION

There isn't much that scares Dr. Jones, but snakes have been his longtime phobia. This area's lower trenches are filled with slithery critters, and Indy cringes in fear whenever a snake is near. Use Sallah to dispatch snakes or find clever ways to avoid them.

B

Use Indy's whip at the whip point here to yank out a ledge. Then switch to Sallah and leap across.

C

Slide the two small Anubis statues here toward the background to discover a pile of jiggling LEGO bits and a torch. Stack the bits to create a fire pit, then light the fire with

the torch. This clears a path through the snakes for Indy; step on both buttons after he crosses to open the way forward.

Artifact Piece 1

Grab a torch and explore the snake pit to discover your first artifact piece in the upper-left corner.

Area 2: Connecting Corridor

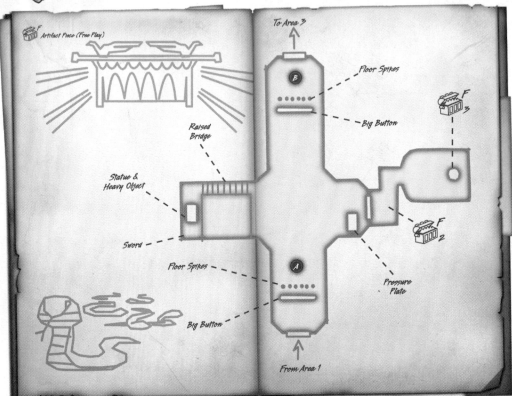

Artifact Piece (Free Play)

To Area 3

Floor Spikes

B

Big Button

Raised Bridge

Statue & Heavy Object

Sword

Floor Spikes

Big Button

A

Pressure Plate

From Area 1

Triggering Traps

After stepping on the large button here, punch the spikes that jut up from the floor to destroy them.

TIP

Use Sallah to dispatch any snakes you encounter while exploring the corridor.

Free Play Goodies

Artifact Piece 2

During Free Play mode, send a tiny character through the little door in this area to reach a ledge beyond the left pit. (You can't lower the bridge to cross this pit during Story mode). Have that little character collect the sword from the ledge, then return through the tiny door.

Once you're back in the main corridor, face the bridge and target its chain. Toss the sword to cut the chain and lower the bridge so you may cross.

After crossing the bridge, swap to a character that possesses the explosion ability and blow up the ledge's silver statues. Now you can pick up and carry the heavy object that was anchored to the statues before.

Free Play Goodies (continued)

Carry the object back across the bridge and set it down on the large pressure switch near the right-side wall. This opens a secret alcove in the wall, beyond which lies an artifact piece.

Artifact Piece 3

After nabbing the previous artifact piece, smash the small vases in the secret alcove to reveal a hidden passage to an odd chamber. Slide this room's movable block along the tiled floor and into place to reveal a spinner. Shove the spinner counter-clockwise as far as it will go to reveal yet another artifact piece. Nice!

Decoding the Ancient Glyphs

Use the blue book you found back in the snake pit area to solve the glyph puzzle on the wall here. It's like a memory game: Watch the pattern as the glyphs light up, then input the same pattern to solve the puzzle and open the door.

TIP

If you don't have the blue book, smash a nearby vase to discover one.

Area 3: Sphinx Chamber

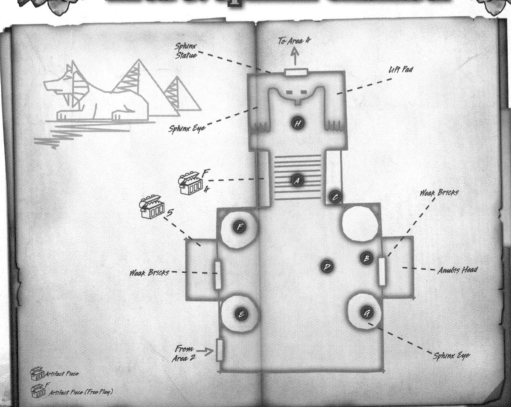

Sphinx Statue

To Area 4

Lift Pad

Sphinx Eye

Sphinx Eye

H

F 4

A

C

Weak Bricks

F

5

B

P

Weak Bricks

Anubis Head

E

G

From Area 2

Sphinx Eye

Artifact Piece

F Artifact Piece (Free Play)

Buggin' Out

Dash up the steps here to collect a key, but watch out: The steps collapse into a slide, and a bunch of scarabs slide down to eat you for lunch! Indy doesn't fear these little pests, so stop each one, then pick up the key.

Insert the key into the mechanism on the wall here, then turn it to reveal some weak bricks. Smash the bricks to reveal a tiny alcove, then stack the jiggling LEGO bits you find within to assemble the head of an Anubis statue.

Place the Anubis head on the small green pad here to complete the statue. This causes the steps to revert to their original, scalable form.

Free Play Goodie

Artifact Piece 4

During Free Play mode, use a character with the explosion ability to destroy the sphinx chamber's silver Anubis statue and reveal a hidden artifact piece.

Riddle of the Sphinx

Find a handle lying on the ground here and place it on the nearby pillar. Then use the handle to rotate the pillar 90 degrees clockwise.

Use the orange handle to rotate this lower-left pillar 90 degrees counterclockwise, then climb up the nearby rope as Indy to reach the top of the pillar. Jump to the next pillar ahead (the one in the room's upper-left corner).

TIP

When airborne, use Indy's shadow to help you land each jump.

Have Indy wait on the pillar and take control of Sallah. Use Sallah to rotate Indy's pillar 90 degrees counterclockwise, so that Indy can use his whip to swing across to the upper-right pillar (which you rotated before).

Once Indy's standing atop the upper-right pillar, have Sallah rotate that pillar back to its original position so Indy can leap to this final pillar, in the room's lower-right corner. Collect the strange object from atop this pillar and then drop to the ground.

Carry the object up the steps and over to the sphinx. Stand on one of the two brown squares on the ground to ride up like an elevator, then place the object in the sphinx's eye. Repeat this with the other eye object (found on the sphinx's right paw) to open a door in the sphinx's chest. Continue to the next area.

Artifact Piece 5

Turn the key jutting out from the sphinx chamber's left wall to reveal some weak bricks. Punch through these blocks to discover a small alcove where an artifact piece is found.

Area 4: Ark Chamber

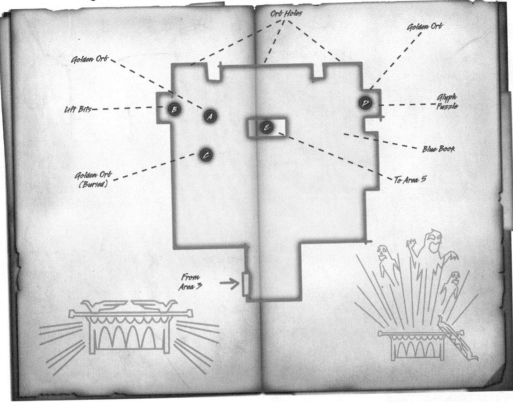

Orb Holes

Golden Orb

Golden Orb

Lift Bits

Glyph
Puzzle

B

A

D

E

Blue Book

C

Golden Orb
(Buried)

To Area 5

From
Area 3

Sacred Ground

At last, Indiana and Sallah have arrived at the heart of the tomb. Find a golden orb on the ground here and insert it into one of the three holes in the background wall.

Smash through the weak bricks here and collect a flat object from within the alcove beyond. Place the object on the pad near the middle of the chamber's background wall to create a lift. Now you can reach the background wall's middle orb hole.

Use Sallah's trusty shovel to excavate another glowing orb from the glowing dirt here. Place this second orb into one of the background wall's holes.

Use your blue book to solve the glyph puzzle in the nook here. Then, as Indy, climb the handrails that emerge from the chamber's right wall to reach the nook's upper ledge. Use Indy's whip to retrieve the glowing orb, then set the orb into the final hole.

TIP

Lost your blue book? Use Sallah's shovel to dig one up from the nearby ground.

When all three golden orbs have been placed, the Ark of the Covenant rises from the room's central dais. Approach the Ark to advance the story.

LEGO **INDIANA JONES**

THE ORIGINAL ADVENTURES

Area 5: Snake Pit Revisited

Back Where We Started

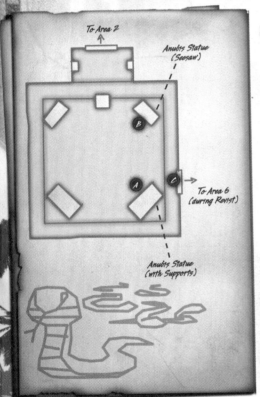

Curse that evil Belloq! He's stolen the Ark, and his wicked associates have cast Marion down into the Well of Souls along with Indy. Marion's your partner now. Use her superior jumping ability to reach the dangling ropes here, near the chamber's lower-right Anubis statue. Grab both ropes with Marion to bring down the statue's wooden supports.

Now have Indy stand atop the upper-right Anubis statue's wooden platform. Switch to Marion again and jump up to grab the rope that's dangling high overhead here. Marion's weight elevates Indy's platform like a seesaw. Switch back to Indy and use his whip to cross over to the lower-right Anubis statue.

With its supports gone, Indy's weight is enough to topple the chamber's lower-right Anubis statue, causing it to smash through the far wall. Cross the fallen statue and proceed through the opening you've made.

Area 6: Secret Passage

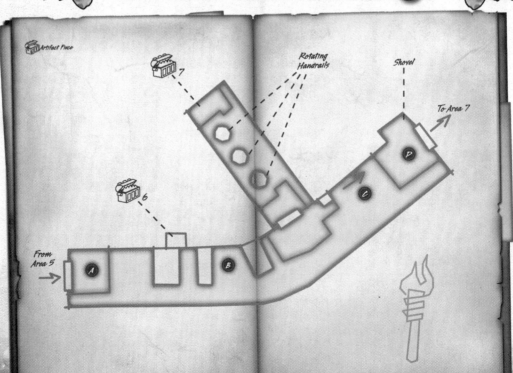

Tread Lightly

Indy and Marion have escaped the snakes, but they're now faced with a treacherous passage full of pitfalls. Stand atop the tallest brick on this first ledge and leap to grab the handrail ahead. Jump and shimmy over to the next ledge.

Exploit Marion's superior jumping skill to navigate this area with less stress.

Swing from the dangling vine here, building momentum so you can jump out and reach the next bit of pathway.

Use Indy's whip to cross this next wide gap, then destroy some spiderwebs in the final ledge's corner to discover a shovel. Use the shovel to dig out a nearby lever, then yank its handle to extend a bridge for Marion.

Jump and hang from one of the final ledge's two ropes, and wait until your other character does the same. When both characters are hanging from the ropes, the door ahead opens. Beware the scarabs that come skittering out!

Artifact Piece 6

Drop to the low ledge near the vine to discover an artifact piece. Use the vine to climb back up.

Artifact Piece 7

Destroy some vases near the passage's midway point to reveal an entrance to a side chamber. Carefully leap along the tiny handrails of the chamber's rotating platforms, making for the artifact piece on the far ledge.

Area 7: Inner Chamber

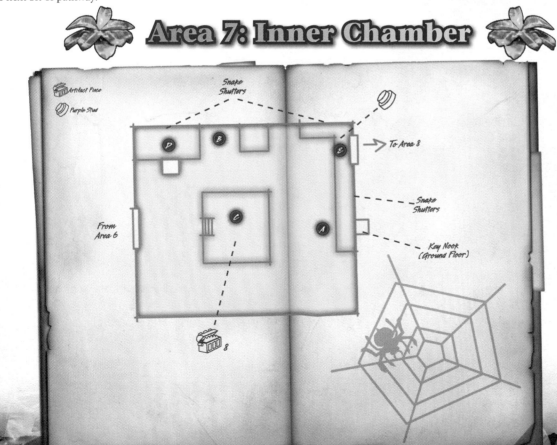

Two Cogs and a Key

Smash the objects at the room's far end to reveal two cogs (one of which lies buried) and some weak bricks. Dig up the buried cog with the shovel you just found, then smash through the bricks to discover a key.

TIP

If you don't have a shovel, return to the previous area to retrieve one.

Place both cogs on the green pad along the background wall and then use the key to turn them. This raises a giant platform, which will soon come in handy.

Stack the jiggling LEGO blocks in the room's center to form a tall, movable block. Don't slide the block anywhere just yet, though; keep it right where it is for now.

As Marion, jump onto this lowest ledge, then begin circling around the chamber's ledges. Stomp any snakes that drop from overhead shutters.

TIP

Jump and hang on the snake shutters' handrails to close them. No snakes will slither out afterward!

TIP

To claim the purple stud from above the second snake shutter, jump off the shutter's handrail before the shutter closes under Marion's weight. You can't reach the purple stud after closing the shutter!

Both Indy and Marion must stand on the buttons here to open the way forward. Indy can't get up here until you build and position the room's central block so he can reach the room's upper ledges.

Artifact Piece 8

As Marion, close all three snake shutters along this chamber's walls by jumping up and hanging onto the shutters' handrails. This reveals a secret artifact at the room's center! Jump from the room's central block to reach this prize.

Area 8: Coffin Corridor

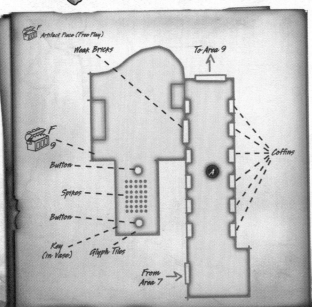

Respecting the Dead

Keep toward the middle of this creepy corridor—if you get too close to many of the sarcophagi that line the walls, spikes fly out to defeat you! Coffins that aren't trapped can be punched for a few studs, but it's a risky venture. All you really need to do here is dash down the center of the hallway to reach the next area.

Free Play Goodie
🗄️🚌 Artifact Piece 9 🚌🗄️

Smash through the weak bricks at the far end of the coffin corridor to reach a large side room. Much of the side room's floor is covered in spikes—step on the button to lower the spikes for a short time, then sprint across. Jump at the end to avoid being jabbed when the spikes pop back up.

Break the vase beyond the spikes to reveal a key, then insert the key into the nearby mechanism. Turn the key to make a ledge pop out from the left wall.

Insert the missing glyphs into the glyph puzzle to complete it. Then use a character that owns the academic ability to solve the puzzle, revealing a hidden artifact piece. Nice work!

Take the set of glyphs from the nearby pedestal and then ride up the lift block to reach the top of the ledge you just revealed. Walk across the ledge to safely bypass the spikes.

Area 9: Viper Lair

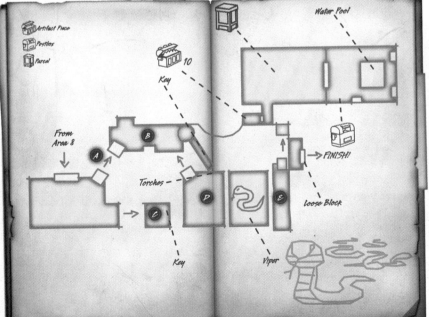

Two Ways to Cross

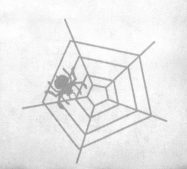

The most obvious way to navigate this chamber is to whip-swing across this first pit as Indy.

Use the shovel you discover at this ledge to dig up some handrail pieces, then stack those bits to form a handrail that leads upward. Scale the handrail and then use Indy's whip a second time to cause a plank to fall and serve as a bridge. Collect a key as you cross the narrow stretch, then drop to the ledge below.

Though it wasn't immediately obvious, you might also have used Marion to navigate this chamber with less ado: A high overhead vine that is totally out of view allows Marion to leap from the starting platform and swing her way onto this hidden ledge, where a second key is found. Take control of Marion and jump onto this ledge to retrieve the key.

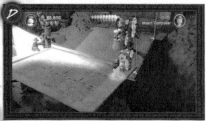

Guide both characters to this ledge and use the two keys you've discovered to raise the platform ahead. Beware: Once the platform is raised, a giant snake drops onto it and attacks!

Showdown: Venomous Viper

The moment the viper appears, use Indy's whip to snatch a torch from the nearby pillar. Then toss the torch at the viper to hurt it. Repeat this with the other torch, then wait until the torches reappear.

The viper spits venom at you in regular intervals. Keep away and stay mobile to avoid these attacks as you wait for the torches to respawn. Snag a torch, avoid the viper's venom, then hurl the torch at it to hurt it. Repeat until the viper collapses into a pile of jiggling LEGO bits, then stack those bits to form a lift.

Exiting the Well with Your Soul

When you're ready to flee this dreadful place, ride up the lift you built out of the viper's remains and then jump to the nearby ledge. Push against the block that sticks out from the wall to find daylight at last. Level complete!

Artifact Piece 10

Before fleeing this area, whip-swing across the gap near the lift you built from the viper's remains to reach a low, corner ledge. Jump from there and grab onto a hanging rope, then climb up.

Jump from the rope to reach a high background nook, where an artifact piece is found.

Parcel

No special skills are require to obtain this level's parcel. After claiming the artifact piece from the high nook, smash apart the nook's yellow canisters to reveal a secret opening in the wall. Dash through to reach a large side room.

Travel to the room's far end, then stack some jiggling LEGO bits to build a postbox. Now you just need to find that parcel!

Stack some more jiggling blocks near the square pool to connect a water flow. Pull a nearby lever to get water flowing into the pool from the adjacent source.

Smash a vase in the room's corner to find a key, then insert the key into the mechanism near the postbox and turn it. This gets even more water flowing into the pool.

When all three water sources have been activated, the pool's water level rises, and the current begins flowing into the distant trenches. This causes flowers to sprout! Smash each of those flowers to reveal the parcel. Then mail the parcel back to Barnett College.

PURSUING THE ARK

Burned by Belloq

As if having one precious artifact stolen away by Belloq wasn't bad enough, Dr. Jones has now lost what could easily be the most incredible archeological find in history. But although Belloq has taken the Ark from Indy, he has yet to transport it out of Cairo. Having escaped the Well of Souls with his life, Indiana Jones is ready to take his revenge. Belloq *will* pay, and the Ark will be recovered!

STAGE COLLECTIBLES

Treasure	Area	Notes	Got It?
1	1	Beyond silver bars (solve glyph puzzle; explosion and academic abilities required)	☐
2	1	On high ledge (tiny size ability required)	☐
3	1	In nook near cart (dig down from above)	☐
4	2	Atop water tower behind silver bars (explosion ability required)	☐
5	2	Behind silver cart (make officer blow it up)	☐
6	2	Atop guard tower (use vehicle to lower platform)	☐
7	2	At swimming hole (build raft; hit duckies)	☐
8	3	From old radio (must build; shovel or excavate ability required)	☐
9	3	Shoot targets with enemy's pistol to reveal (only doable in Free Play)	☐
10	4	In back of jeep (collect before jeep crashes)	☐
▯	1	On ledge atop crane (explosion ability required)	☐

True Adventurer stud requirement:
47,000 studs

Helpful Free Play Skills:
- Academic ability
- Excavate ability
- Explosion ability
- Tiny size ability

STORY MODE CHARACTERS

Indiana Jones (Desert)

Marion (Evening Dress)

Sallah (Desert)

Area 1: Excavation Site A

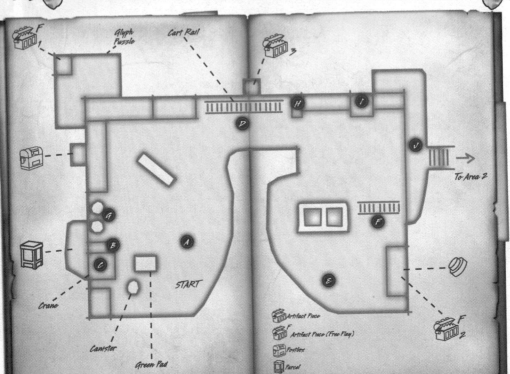

F 1
Glyph Puzzle
Cart Rail
3
H
I
D
J
To Area 2
G
B
F
A
C
START
E
Crane
Canister
Green Pad

Artifact Piece
F Artifact Piece (Free Play)
Postbox
Parcel
Purple Stud
F 2

Crane Game

A

Secure the area near the start point, then place a nearby box of LEGO bits onto the green pad in front of the crane.

CAUTION

Belloq's excavation site is crawling with armed guards. Steal their weaponry and use it against them!

B

Use Indy's whip to yank down a ladder here, then climb up and retrieve a second box of LEGO bits. Place this object on the green pad as well, then stack the jiggling bits to assemble the crane's hook.

C

Pilot the crane and use its hook to lift the giant cylindrical canister that's within reach. Pivot the crane in a counterclockwise fashion and drop the canister on the raised, circular platform next to the crane.

Free Play Goodies

Parcel

After fixing the crane, use it to grab your other character and drop them on the high wooden platform to the left. This allows the character to reach the parcel on the ledge behind the crane. Collect the parcel and carry it down to the ground.

Continued on next page

Free Play Goodies (continued)

Toggle your Free Play character to someone who has the explosion ability, then destroy the silver bars below the right-side scaffolding. Pull the lever in the nook to raise some stone steps and remove the bars that block the postbox above.

Quickly collect the parcel, then hop up the stone steps. Place the parcel in the postbox to mail it back to Barnett College. You must do this before time runs out and the bars slam closed once more. If you don't quite make it, leave the parcel right near the postbox, then drop down and pull the lever again. Now you can quickly reach the postbox and deposit the parcel!

Artifact Piece 1

Use a character who has the explosion ability to destroy the silver bars at the upper-left corner of the site. Toggle your Free Play character to one with the academic ability and solve the glyph puzzle in the area beyond. This reveals a hidden artifact piece! Toggle back to your explosion-ability character and destroy the glass case surrounding the artifact piece so you may claim your prize.

Free Play Goodies (continued)

Artifact Piece 2

Shove the mine cart at the site's far-right side into the wall, then stack the jiggling bits that remain to form a tiny door in the wall. Toggle to a tiny character and crawl through the door to reach a high ledge where an artifact piece and purple stud are found.

Fixing the Cart Rail

After playing with the crane, dash over here to find a stretch of cart rail in disrepair. Three sections of the track are missing. The first bit of track is nearby; pick it up and place it on the rail.

TIP

Smash barrels full of tools to find shovels, then use a shovel to dig up the chests that are buried about the site. Next, whack open each chest for studs!

Find a shovel, then use it to dig up the LEGO bits that are buried here. Stack those bits to form another section of track.

Push against the mine cart here, at the site's far-right side, until it flies off the track and slams into the wall. Stack the jiggling bits that remain to form a tiny door and the third and final piece of missing track. (See the artifact piece two text for details on the tiny door.)

On with the Chase

With the northern rail fully repaired, return to the crane and leap up the cylindrical canisters as Marion. Cross the wooden scaffolding ledges that follow and jump to land on top of the rail cart. Switch control to Indy and shove the cart to the left so that Marion can reach the next portion of scaffolding ahead.

Stack the jiggling pile of LEGO bits on the scaffolding beyond the rail cart to assemble a rope. Now it's much easier to climb back up here if you happen to fall.

Jump up and grab onto one of the two hanging ropes here. Your partner automatically does the same, causing a wide board to fall and form a footbridge. Cross the board to reach the far ledge.

You're home free! Simply scamper up the steps here to reach the next area.

🏺 Artifact Piece 3 🏺

After you've repaired the cart rail, equip Marion with a shovel and then guide her along the scaffolding to the top of the movable cart. Switch to Indy and shove the cart halfway along its rail, then change back to Marion and leap onto the tiny background ledge. Start digging until Marion tunnels down into a lower nook, where an artifact piece is found.

Area 2: Excavation Site B

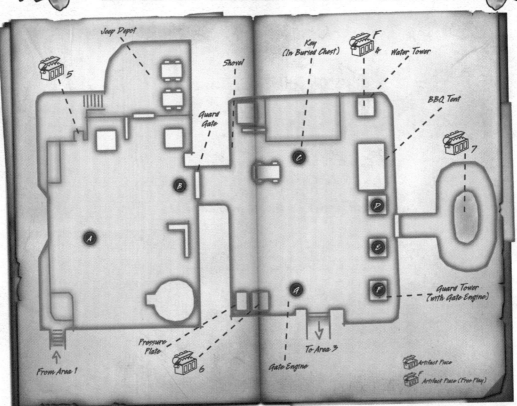

Master of Disguise

Indy and Marion fall under heavy attack in this area: endless armed soldiers stream forth to combat them. Dangerous officers appear from time to time as well; they toss explosive potato mashers all about. Avoid these boom-sticks at all costs!

TIP

To access the jeep depot beyond the area's north gate, use Marion's great jumping ability to leap onto the high left ledge. Then dash north, sprinting down the far steps to reach the jeeps. These vehicles are powerful enough to ram through the depot gate and crush enemies, but they won't help you get past the reinforced guard gate to the right.

To advance, you must fool the guard at this gate into letting you pass. Defeat a potato masher-hurling officer, then swipe his hat to disguise yourself. Knock on the guard post window so the guard can ID you, then hurry through the gate after he opens it.

Buried Treasure

Things start to quiet down once you're past the guard gate. Find a shovel by destroying a nearby barrel full of tools, then excavate a chest from the sparkling ground here. Bash open the chest afterward to find a key—it's best if Marion collects it.

Free Play Goodie

🎮🏺 Artifact Piece 4 🏺🎮

Destroy the grills inside the BBQ tent at the area's right side to find two ladder pieces. Bring the two ladder pieces to the nearby water tower to build a ladder leading up to the top.

Climb the ladder you've built and toggle your Free Play character to someone with the ability to create explosions. Blow up the silver bars surrounding the artifact piece at the top of the water tower, then claim your prize.

Opening the South Gate

Climb onto the guard tower near the BBQ tent. Pull the overhead rope to make some LEGO bits fall from above, then stack the bits to complete the tower's key mechanism.

Turn the key to send a mobile rope on an overhead wire rolling to the right.

Switch to whichever character is carrying the key you found inside the buried chest, then jump up and grab onto the mobile rope as it slowly reels back to the left. Quickly jump off of the rope, landing on the next guard tower ahead. Use your key on this tower's mechanism to advance the next mobile rope, then use that rope to reach the far-right guard tower.

Pull the lever you find atop this far-right guard tower to lower a vital object to the ground—a gate engine. Set this object into place at one side of the locked south gate.

The other gate engine is much easier to find. Just stack the jiggling blocks near the gate to build it. Place this second engine to open the gate so you may continue to the next area.

🏺 Artifact Piece 5 🏺

If you're really slick, you can trick an enemy officer into destroying the silver water cart near the jeep depot with one of his potato mashers. With the cart out of the way, you're free to claim an artifact piece from the tiny nook beyond. You must stand near the cart and bait an officer into blasting the cart for you, though. If this is proving too difficult, know that you can always replay this level in Free Play mode and use a character who has the explosion ability to obliterate the water cart instead.

🏺 Artifact Piece 6 🏺

Have Indy drive a vehicle (jeep or Rolls Royce) onto the large pressure plate near the southern gate to lower the platform of the nearby guard tower. Switch to Marion and leap onto the platform, then jump up to grab an artifact piece that's hovering near the top of the tower.

🏺 Artifact Piece 7 🏺

Drive a vehicle straight through the site's far-right gate to visit a tiny oasis. Destroy the patio furniture around the swimming hole here to reveal some jiggling bits that form a raft when stacked.

Backtrack and grab a shovel from the site if you don't have one at hand, then board the raft. A number of rubber duckies emerge from the water's surface. Paddle the raft in a circle, ramming into each ducky in turn. Dunk all of the duckies to reveal a secret artifact piece that hovers just above the water!

Area 3: Airfield

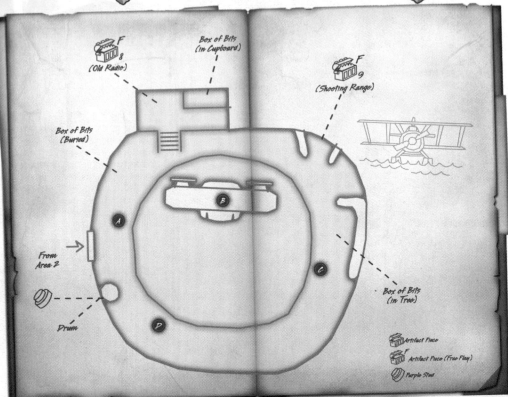

Showdown: Enemy Boxer

Indy and Marion arrive at the airfield just in time to witness the Ark being hauled away by truck. An enemy boxer must be defeated before the pair can give chase, but this guy's too much for Indy's fists to handle. Instead of throwing down like normal, pick up an anvil from this spot and carry it toward the boxer.

TIP

The enemy boxer won't chase you outside the airfield's circular landing zone, so feel free to run about in search of hearts and studs.

Free Play Goodies

Artifact Piece 8

Three boxes of LEGO bits are hidden about the airfield. One box is in a tree (destroy the tree to reveal it). Another is in the background hut's cupboard (punch the cupboard open to find it). The third is buried in the sand near the anvil. There are no shovels at the airfield, so you can only dig up this final box of bits during Free Play mode, with a character who has the excavate ability. (Assuming you aren't still carrying a shovel from a previous area.)

Place all three boxes of LEGO bits on the green pad near the background hut, then stack the jiggling LEGO bits to form an old-time radio that plays a jazzy tune. Moments later, an artifact piece appears!

Artifact Piece 9

Revisit this level in Free Play mode to find the shooting range in the airfield's upper-right corner up and running. Use a character that carries a firearm by default to shoot the targets when they spin around. Hit all of the targets to reveal a secret artifact piece!

Unfair Fight

The boxer attempts to punch through the anvil, but that doesn't quite work out! He only injures his fist, losing some health in the process.

A truckload of enemy soldiers tears onto the scene after the boxer punches the anvil. Quickly pilot the airfield's central jet, turning its guns loose on the soldiers. (The jet can't harm the boxer.)

TIP

Use the jet's guns to blast open the tall drum near the gate and reveal a valuable purple stud!

Obliterate the enemy truck with the jet's guns, then hop out and stack the truck's jiggling remains to form another anvil. Carry this one toward the boxer, too. He punches it and loses another heart.

Again, shortly after the boxer has injured himself on the anvil, another truck full of enemy soldiers speeds into the area. Pilot the jet once more, destroy the truck with your guns, and then stack the truck's remains to form a third anvil. Carry this toward the boxer to make him punch it. You win the fight. Sallah then pulls up in a truck and Indy and Marion climb aboard. The three speed off in pursuit of the Ark.

Area 4: Truck Chase

Follow that Ark!

An enemy truck pulls up next to Indiana and Sallah (your new partner for this segment). Jump onto the enemy truck's roof and defeat the soldiers that climb up to attack. After defeating the truck's driver, hop into the driver's seat, press the Jump button to hit the gas, and speed toward the next group of trucks ahead.

Keep fighting soldiers on top of each group of trucks you catch up to, defeating the drivers so you can speed toward the next convoy ahead. Eventually, Indy and Sallah catch up to the truck that's carrying the Ark.

After dealing with the waves of enemy soldiers, leap to the Ark transport truck and take out its driver. Climb into the truck's driver's seat and put the pedal to the metal. Indy rams into Belloq's Rolls Royce, sending it flying off the road. Level complete!

Artifact Piece 10

Keep your eyes peeled while battling atop the trucks: A smaller truck pulls up behind the third convoy, and it's carrying an artifact piece! Quickly jump aboard and claim this precious cargo before the truck crashes (you may need to use a double-jump to clear the distance).

OPENING THE ARK

Waylaid at Sea

Dr. Jones's heroic efforts to recover the Ark were shockingly successful, but the sweet taste of victory didn't last very long. Belloq and his wicked associates caught up with Indy while they were ferrying the Ark away by ship, and the forces of evil have once again reclaimed the Ark—and taken Marion hostage! In a last-ditch effort, Indiana managed to sneak aboard the enemy submarine. He and Marion now find themselves trapped in the heart of enemy terriorty!

STAGE COLLECTIBLES

Treasure	Area	Notes	Got It?
1	1	Destroy sub's silver valves (explosion ability required)	☐
2	1	On high left ledge (tiny size ability required)	☐
3	1	In room beyond guard post (use motorboat to reach)	☐
4	1	Underwater beneath walkway (swim underwater to collect)	☐
5	2	Buried in stable (excavation ability required)	☐
6	2	In birthday room (use Indy to fool guard at guard post)	☐
7	2	In right bunker (use left bunker's buttons to access)	☐
8	3	In cave behind glyph puzzle (academic ability required)	☐
9	3	Dig up camera with a shovel; push to reveal	☐
10	3	In cave beyond Ark (smash crate and dig up)	☐
	2	In secret room (solve glyph puzzle and room puzzle; academic ability required)	☐

True Adventurer stud requirement: 40,000 studs

Helpful Free Play Skills:

Academic ability

Excavate ability

Explosion ability

Tiny size ability

STORY MODE CHARACTERS

Indiana Jones (Army Disguise)

Marion (Nightgown)

Area 1: Submarine Pen

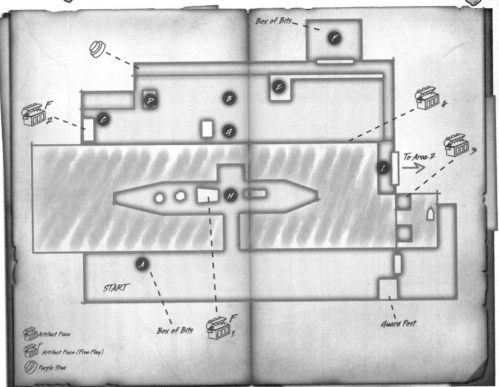

Box of Bits

To Area 2

START

Box of Bits

Guard Post

Artifact Piece

Artifact Piece (Free Play)

Purple Stud

Subs and Such

There must be a way out of this dank submarine station! Collect a box of LEGO bits from the ground here and place it on the sub where indicated.

Use Indy's whip at the whip point here to reveal a ladder. Climb up to reach the ledge above.

Storming the Office

Jump onto the hanging platform here, then switch to Marion. Turn the key on the background wall below to shuttle Indy over to a distant walkway.

Swim to the opposite side of the pen and jump out onto the walkway. Defeat the patrolling soldiers.

Free Play Goodies

Artifact Piece 1

Use a character that has the explosion ability to destroy the two silver valves at the left end of the sub. This reveals two buttons; step on them both to reveal a hidden artifact piece on top of the sub!

Artifact Piece 2

Toggle your Free Play character to one who's tiny enough to crawl through the little door on the far-left ledge. You pop out from another door on an even higher ledge; claim the artifact piece you discover up here.

Push against the handle on the wall here to grab it, then pull. This lowers a nearby ladder so that both characters can easily reach this high walkway.

Wait for Marion to join you on the walkway, then pull one of the two levers against the wall. Marion automatically pulls the other, and a shutter door opens, granting you access to this office. Ransack the office to find another box of LEGO bits.

Carry the box of bits to this spot. Marion automatically turns the nearby key, causing a floating platform to advance. Step onto the platform to ride over to the sub.

Big Gun

Drop the box here, then stack the jiggling bits to assemble a giant gun. Man the gun and fire at the green halves of the two large spinners in the background wall. Rotate both spinners multiple times to extend a ladder up the wall between them.

Climb the ladder to reach a high walkway near the ceiling. Run along the walkway and exit the submarine pen through the large opening here.

Search the opposite end of the ceiling walkway to discover a hidden purple stud!

Artifact Piece 3

Indy is disguised as an enemy soldier throughout this level, and this lets you fool the guard at the window in the submarine pen's lower-right corner. Knock on the window, and the guard grants you access to the room beyond.

Smash some crates in the room's corner to discover some jiggling LEGO bits, then stack those bits to add a motor to the nearby boat. Steer the motorboat over to the far ledge, then jump out to collect the ledge's artifact piece.

Artifact Piece 4

Swim to the upper-right corner of the submarine pen and spy an underwater artifact piece hidden just below the walkway. This one's easy: just swim underwater and collect your prize!

Area 2: Soldier Compound

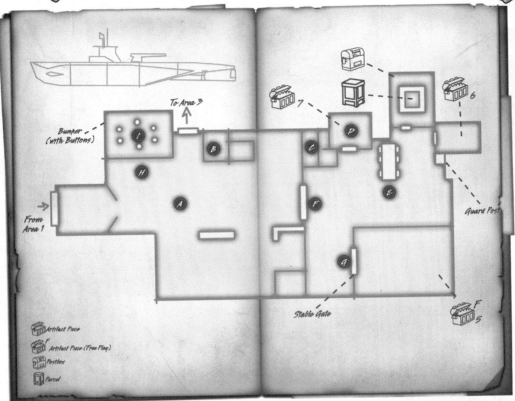

Bunker (with Buttons)

To Area 3

From Area 1

Guard Post

Stable Gate

Artifact Piece
Artifact Piece (Free Play)
Postbox
Parcel

More Guards

Hurry and dispatch the surrounding enemy troops to secure the left half of this outdoor compound.

Use Indy's whip a second time to swing across the next gap and land on this ledge. Stack the jiggling bits you discover here to form a handrail so that Marion can join you.

Dispatch the many soldiers and officer here to secure the area, then use your wrench to fix the nearby broken truck.

Stand on the whip point here and use Indy's whip to drop a crate full of LEGO bits. Stack the bits to build a handrail leading up to another whip point above.

Hitching a Ride

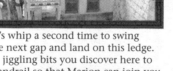

Defeat two soldiers on this rooftop and collect the wrench they were guarding.

The truck is the only vehicle large enough to ram through the gate that separates the two halves of the compound. Smash through the gate, then climb out of the truck.

Free Play Goodies
⚔️🤠 Artifact Piece 5 🤠⚔️

Search the horse stable to discover a sparkling patch of soil. Dig here during Free Play mode to unearth a secret artifact piece!

💼💼 Parcel 💼💼

After repairing the truck, drive a short distance to reveal a glyph puzzle on the wall behind where the truck was parked. Solve the glyph puzzle with a character that has the academic ability to reveal a nearby passage to a secret room!

Smash the crate in the secret room, then stack the jiggling bits that remain to restore the missing floor tiles. Now you can slide both of the large pyramid-shaped objects along the tiles.

Free Play Goodies (continued)

After sliding the pyramids, run up one of the stone ramps and jump on top of one of the pyramids. This lowers its top; wait until your partner does the same. When both pyramid tops are held down, the floor below retracts, revealing the level's parcel! Collect this prize and slot it into the nearby postbox to send it off to Barnett College.

Horsing Around

Return to the right side of the compound and hang from one of the ropes near the horse stable gate. Wait for your partner to hang from the other rope. The gate then opens.

Ride the horse over to this bunker, then press the Jump button. The horse bucks you off; steer your character through the air and onto the top of the bunker. Repeat this with the other character so that both are standing atop the bunker.

Shove the large object along the tiles on the bunker's roof, positioning it onto one

of the roof's seven buttons. Pick up the nearby basket and set it down on the middle button.

Notice the pattern that you're forming on the large background wall as you activate the buttons. Position Indy and Marion so that they complete the pattern, as shown on the nearby brown billboard.

If you set the basket down on an incorrect button, punch the basket to destroy it. Another will soon appear so you can try again.

Completing the pattern opens the bunker door below. Drop down and enter the bunker to acquire a few bazookas. Use these explosive weapons to destroy the nearby silver gate, then dash through to reach the final showdown against Belloq.

🤠 Artifact Piece 6 🤠

Knock on the window of the guard post at the compound's right side. Indy's disguise fools the guard and he raises the nearby gate.

Surprise! The room beyond the gate is all decorated, and a giant cake sits in the middle. Looks like the men were planning a birthday party for their commanding officer. Smash the cake to reveal a hidden artifact piece. You're watching your diet anyway, right?

❧ Artifact Piece 7 ❧

You recreated the billboard pattern atop the bunker to get at those bazookas. But did you notice the other pattern on the door at the compound's right side? Use the bunker buttons to recreate this other pattern (which sort of resembles a candy cane) to open that door, then head inside to nab an artifact piece!

Area 3: Ceremony Grounds

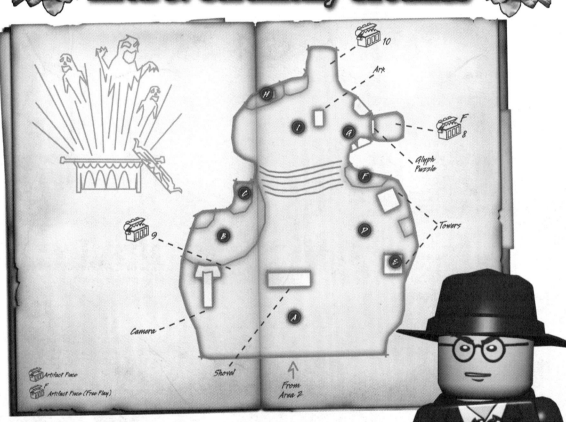

 Artifact Piece

Artifact Piece (Free Play)

Showdown: Belloq

Indy wouldn't destroy the Ark when he had the chance, but nothing will stop him from destroying the forces of evil! Beat down the initial mob of enemy soldiers that attacks you here, then begin exploring the area.

Soldiers will regularly appear to challenge you here. Keep alert!

A Woman's Touch

Pick up the large piece of equipment here and place it on the nearby green pad. Switch to Marion and leap from the top of the equipment so you can grab the handrail on the ledge above.

Marion's the better character to use when chasing after Belloq at first. She's better than Indy at leaping about.

Leap over to this ledge, where Belloq awaits in full ceremonial garb. Quickly punch Belloq before he hits you. The villain doesn't like being hit and flees to another ledge that's currently out of reach.

Stack the jiggling LEGO bits here to attach a metal object to the area's far right wall. Then climb the nearby ladder to reach the top of a tall tower.

Once Marion stands atop this tower, Indy automatically jumps up and grabs a nearby rope. This lowers the metal object you attached to the wall, changing it into a platform. Leap across to reach Belloq's ledge.

Again, punch Belloq the minute you land on his ledge to send him running off. Drop from the ledge and dash up the steps in pursuit.

Free Play Goodie
Artifact Piece 8

Use a character with academic ability to solve the glyph puzzle on the wall near the Ark to gain access to the shallow cave beyond. There you find an artifact piece!

Indiana's Revenge

Indy must be the one to chase Belloq from now on. Hop up these rocks, then make a long jump over to the large rock ahead. Jump from there to grab a nearby rope, then swing onto the handrails that follow.

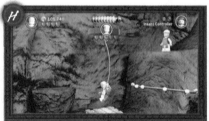

Cross the handrails to reach this ledge, where you discover a whip point. Use Indy's whip to pull down an overhead platform. Now you can leap up to Belloq's ledge. Do so and give Belloq a mouthful of Indy's fist!

Belloq drops from the ledge but finally makes his stand near the Ark. Chase after him and finish the fight with a few fists of fury. Story complete! Sit back and enjoy the ending.

Artifact Piece 9

Find a shovel near the southern crates and use it to excavate some jiggling LEGO bits near the narrow strip of floor tiles to the right. Stack the bits to form a camera, then shove the camera along the tiles as far as it will go. The camera kicks on when it reaches the far end, revealing a hidden artifact piece!

Artifact Piece 10

Bash apart the crates in the nook beyond the Ark to reveal a patch of glimmering soil. Use the shovel you found near the southern crates to excavate an artifact piece!

SHANGHAI SHOWDOWN

Anything Goes

Dr. Jones's adventures have led him far. Our intrepid adventurer now finds himself in a classy Shanghai club: a carefully chosen public setting for a dangerous meeting with some very wily villains. Indiana's purpose here is to trade an invaluable piece of Chinese history for a priceless diamond. Unfortunately for Indy, these wicked Chinese mobsters have other plans!

STAGE COLLECTIBLES

Item	Area	Notes	Got It?
1	1	Above drum set (push kick drum and jump off)	☐
2	1	Destroy 3 silver tables with gong to reveal	☐
3	2	On ledge above glyph puzzle (explosion and academic abilities required)	☐
4	2	In far-left alcove (explosion and excavate abilities required)	☐
5	2	On far-left awning (thuggee chant ability required)	☐
6	2	On high ledge near first car part (use Short Round)	☐
7	2	On high awning above gate (bounce up the awnings)	☐
8	2	On high rooftop ledge	☐
9	3	In parcel area (explosion and enemy disguise abilities required)	☐
10	3	On high ledge near forklift (use forklift to reach)	☐
	3	Beyond left gate (explosion ability required)	☐

True Adventurer stud requirement: 52,000 studs

Helpful Free Play Skills:

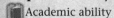 Academic ability

Enemy Disguise

Excavate ability

Explosion ability

Super jump ability

Thuggee chant ability

STORY MODE CHARACTERS

Indiana Jones (Dinner Suit)

Willie

Short Round

Indiana Jones

Area 1: Club Obi-Wan

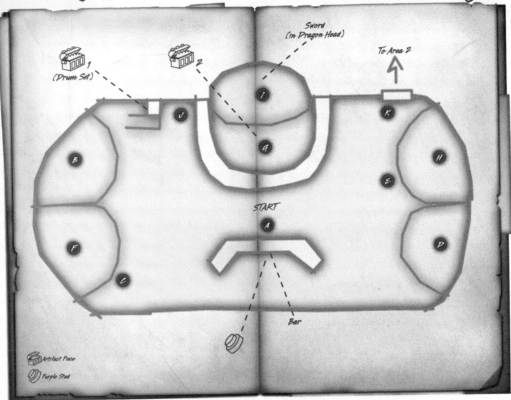

1 (Drum Set)

2

Sword (In Dragon Head)

To Area 2

START

Bar

Artifact Piece

Purple Stud

You Keep the Girl; I'll Find Another

Oh no! Indy has been poisoned by Lao Che, whose goons have fled with the antidote. Indy isn't of much use while doubled up in agony; switch to Willie and snatch the large diamond off the nearby table.

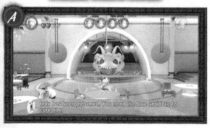

Lao Che's men have fled to the club's high balconies. Toss the diamond at the mobster on this balcony, who currently has the

antidote Indy needs. The man quickly passes the antidote to an associate so he can catch the diamond.

The Second Diamond

Step on the two buttons here to open the nearby cabinet. Take the diamond you discover inside.

Toss the second diamond to the mobster on this balcony. The man passes the antidote and catches the diamond.

The Third Diamond

Stand in front of the glass cabinet here and use Willie's unique scream ability to shatter the glass. (Just keep screaming until it shatters.) Snatch the diamond from the cabinet.

Hurl the third diamond at the man on this balcony to make him pass the antidote across the room. (These guys are getting rich here!)

The Fourth Diamond

The final diamond is hidden among the balloons near the ceiling in the middle of the club. Jump up and grab the dangling rope to loose the balloons, then pop them all to find the diamond (and a lot of studs).

Toss the diamond to the final mobster, who stands atop this balcony. The man drops the antidote to catch the diamond, and Indy dives to catch the vial before it shatters on the floor.

Let's Get Gong-ing

Indy's back in action, and not a moment too soon. Stand on the two buttons atop the

stage here to open the jaws of the dragon head prop. Collect the sword you discover inside the dragon's mouth.

Stand in front of the large hanging gong here and target its chain. Toss the sword to cut the chain, freeing the giant gong.

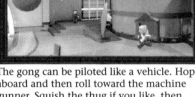

The gong can be piloted like a vehicle. Hop aboard and then roll toward the machine gunner. Squish the thug if you like, then roll through the nearby window to make a daring escape from the club.

🎲 Artifact Piece 1 🎲

Shove the large kick drum in the club's far-left corner over to the rest of the drum

set. Then jump atop the kick drum as Willie and leap up to grab the artifact piece hovering high above. (You must use Willie because she's a superior jumper.)

🎲 Artifact Piece 2 🎲

While rolling about in the gong, smash through the three silver tables in the club to reveal a hidden artifact piece near the stage!

Area 2: Shanghai Streets

Searching for Parts

Indy and crew need to fix their car so they can flee Shanghai. Smash the boxes here to reveal a tiny door, then switch to Short Round and crawl through to reach a high ledge.

Use a handrail and rope to reach this high ledge, where you discover a missing part of the car. Carry the car part to the car and set it down where indicated. One more part to find!

As Indy or Short Round, climb the dangling rope here to reach the ledge above. Cross the ledge until you reach a gap you can't jump.

Map on next page!

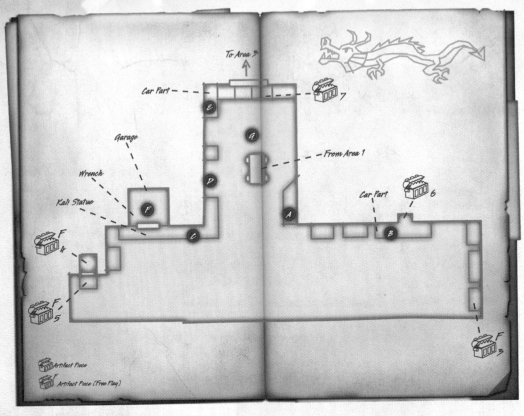

When you reach this gap, switch to Willie, then jump up and grab the high overhead rope. This pulls down an awning, allowing the character above to continue along the ledge. Repeat this when you reach the next gap.

The other car part sits here, at the far end of the ledge. Grab it and place it near the car, then stack the mass of jiggling bits to return the vehicle to its proper form.

Free Play Goodies

Artifact Piece 3

Destroy the silver objects in the area's far-right corner to reveal some jiggling LEGO bits. Stack the bits to form a tiny door on the wall, then send Short Round (or any other tiny character) crawling through.

The tiny character pops out of another door on a ledge above. Jump into the small nearby bucket, then switch to your other character.

Toggle the character in the street to one who has the academic ability, then solve the nearby glyph puzzle to reveal a key mechanism in a hidden nook. Turn the key to ferry the tiny character in the bucket across the overhead gap so they may collect an artifact piece from an otherwise unreachable ledge.

Free Play Goodies (continued)

⚔ 👤 Artifact Piece 4 👤 🧪

Have a character with the excavate ability dig up a heavy object from the far-left flower bed near the garage. Toggle to a character with the explosion ability and blow up the nearby silver gate, then place the heavy object on the pressure plate beyond. This reveals a secret artifact piece!

✋ 👤 Artifact Piece 5 👤 ✋

Use a character who has the thuggee chant ability to activate the Kali statue on the ledge above the garage. Wait for a balloon to float by, then grab its string. Let the balloon carry you over to a distant awning, where an artifact piece awaits discovery.

Fleeing the Streets

The car is now fully assembled, but it still needs to be repaired. Beat up the gangsters that rush from the nearby garage to attack you, then enter the garage. Collect a wrench from within, then return to repair the car.

After fixing the car, hop in and flip a 180. Smash through the background gate to reach the next area.

👤 Artifact Piece 6 👤

While visiting this ledge as Short Round to retrieve the first car part, smash the objects to reveal some jiggling LEGO bits, then stack them to form a door. The door swings open, revealing a hidden artifact piece!

👤 Artifact Piece 7 👤

After crossing the ledge to collect the second car part, bounce along the awnings to the right to reach an artifact piece on an awning high above.

Area 3: Hangar

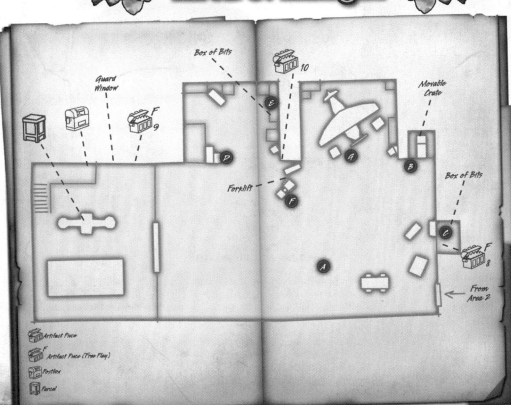

Fight, then Flight

Lao Che's goons are all over the hangar, so be prepared to fight! Take out the first few groups to secure the area.

Use Willie to reach this high ledge, then shove the movable crate off the edge. Stack the jiggling bits that spill out after the crate breaks to form a tiny door on the wall, then send Short Round crawling through.

The tiny door brings Short Round to this high rooftop. Smash the crates up here to find a box of LEGO bits. Bring these bits down to the ground and place them near the plane where indicated.

Building the Propeller

Switch to Indy and leap up the stacked crates here to reach the top of the hangar's shelves. Jump to the nearby shelf against the background wall, then use Indy's whip to cross a wide gap.

Indy's antics have led him to a second box of bits, which sits atop this tall shelf. Place these bits in front of the plane as you did before, then stack the bits afterward to assemble the plane's main propeller.

Free Play Goodies
Artifact Piece 8

After sending Short Round through the tiny door and up to the rooftop, toggle your Free Play character to any female, then use her super jump ability to nab the artifact piece from the ledge above.

Parcel

Use a character possessing the explosion ability to destroy the silver crate near the hangar's far-left wall. Collect the sword that was in the crate, then throw the sword at the red rope overhead to open the area's large left gate.

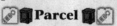

This level's parcel sits on an odd platform in the area beyond the gate. Grab the rope that dangles from the platform to start it spinning, then jump off and climb the nearby steps. Leap from the ledge near the postbox and land atop the spinning platform to collect the parcel. Then mail it back to Barnett College.

Free Play Goodies (continued)
Artifact Piece 9

Use a character who features the enemy disguise ability to fool the guard at the window near the postbox. The guard opens a nearby door, revealing an artifact piece!

Nice Try, Lao Che

Pilot the forklift located here as either Short Round or Willie, and Indy will automatically leap aboard. Drive to the plane and use the forklift to elevate Indy onto the tall whip points.

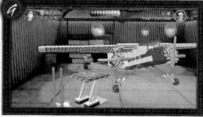

While standing atop the whip points, use Indy's whip to start the plane's pair of side propellers spinning. Indy and friends make their escape once all of the plane's propellers have been activated. Level complete!

Artifact Piece 10

Use the forklift to elevate a character up to a high ledge between the two hangars, right above the forklift's original position. There's an artifact piece up on that ledge!

PANKOT SECRETS

A People in Need

Having narrowly escaped Lao Che's devious "one-way ticket" out of Shanghai, Indiana Jones, Willie, and Short Round find themselves drifting downstream in a lifeboat, lost somewhere near central India. Luckily, the trio is eventually rescued by a tribe of peaceful natives—but Dr. Jones soon discovers that these people have been suffering under terrible oppression. The village elder tells Indy that a secret cult based out of a nearby palace has stolen away all of the villagers' children—along with a sacred stone of great importance. Indiana agrees to help these poor people and sets off to investigate the mysterious cult without delay.

STAGE COLLECTIBLES

Treasure	Area	Notes	Got It?
1	1	In brush near start	☐
2	1	Buried across river (use raft to reach)	☐
3	1	Buried across pit (whip-swing to reach)	☐
4	2	In alcove near Kali statue (smash potted plant)	☐
5	2	In armoire in Indy's bedroom	☐
6	2	In Willie's bedroom, high above bed	☐
7	3	In nook near first pit (jump from vine)	☐
8	3	Near doorway beyond first pit	☐
9	3	In alcove beyond bug pit (destroy skeleton)	☐
10	3	In vases/crates just beyond bug pit door	☐
▯	2	On high ledge near dinner table (thuggee chant ability required to post)	☐

True Adventurer stud requirement:
60,000 studs

Helpful Free Play Skills:
✋ Thuggee chant ability

STORY MODE CHARACTERS

Indiana Jones **Willie** **Short Round**

Area 1: Jungle Approach

Passage by Pachyderm

It's a long way to Pankot Palace and there's no time to lose. Collect the nearby shovel for future use, then climb onto one of the two elephants that have been provided to you by the villagers.

The jungle's mud pools are thick and deep—deep enough to drown in. Cross this first one by elephant, then punch the nearby wooden box to free a vine so your two companions can follow.

CAUTION

Keep alert when smashing objects in the jungle. Vicious little spiders often come skittering out! This is especially troubling for Willie, who's as scared of bugs as Indy is of snakes. Little Short Round happens to be the bravest of the bunch!

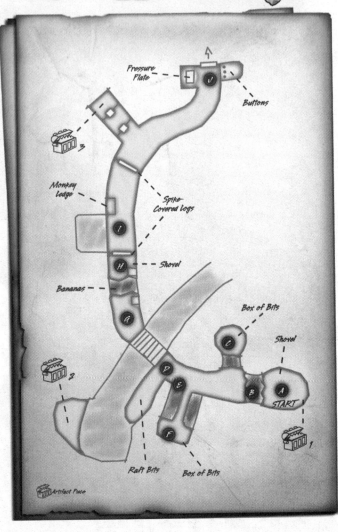

Cross another mud pit to reach this little clearing. Use your elephant to pick up the box of LEGO bits you discover here, then backtrack across the mud.

Place the box of bits on the green pad in front of the raised bridge here. One more box to find!

Lowering the Bridge

Switch to Willie and jump onto the handrail here. Shimmy across the handrail to get past the pit full of snakes below, which even elephants won't mess with.

Stack the jiggling bits you find here to form a handle. Push against the handle to grab it, then pull to extend a footbridge across the snake pit. Now you can carry the nearby box of LEGO bits over to the bridge.

Stack the jiggling bits you've dropped near the bridge to form a whip point. Now Indy can use his whip to lower the bridge!

Lifting the Logs

Return to your elephant and trudge across the bridge. Stomp the spiders in front of the mud pit here, then use the shovel you found near the start to dig up a key from the nearby glowing soil.

There's another shovel just beyond the mud pit if you need it.

Use Indy's whip to swing across the mud pit so your two companions can ride their elephants across. Use the key you found at the mechanism here to raise the spike-covered log.

Mon-Key Business

After raising the spiked log, whip-swing back across the pit, then use Indy's whip to snag a banana from the tree above the mud pit. Cross the mud pit again and continue along the path.

Toss your banana at the monkey on the high ledge beyond the spike-covered log. The monkey gladly throws down the key it was playing with in return. Use your newfound key to raise the next spike-covered log ahead.

Palace Gate

To open the gate, first guide an elephant onto the large pressure plate here. The creature's weight is enough to raise the gate's portcullis, but you still need to unbar the door.

Jump the low wall across from the pressure plate and stand on one of the three buttons. Your companions automatically do the same. When all three buttons are down, the door to the palace becomes unbarred. Dash through to reach the next area.

⚜ Artifact Piece 1 ⚜

This one's an easy find. Search the brush right near the start point to find an artifact piece hidden in plain sight.

⚜ Artifact Piece 2 ⚜

Collect the shovel that stands near the start point, then stack the jiggling LEGOs on the shore near the bridge to form a raft. Hop aboard and paddle over to the left shore, then use your shovel to dig up an artifact piece that's buried underground.

⚜ Artifact Piece 3 ⚜

Outfit Indy with a shovel, then whip-swing across the pit that's not far from the palace gate. Dig up at the glowing soil across the pit to discover a buried artifact piece.

Area 2: Pankot Palace

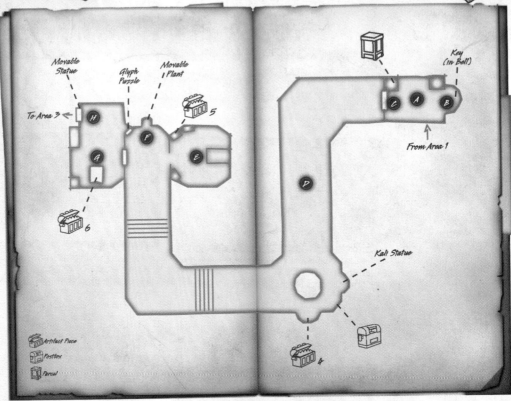

Movable Statue

Glyph Puzzle

Movable Plant

To Area 3 ←

H

F

5

G

E

6

Parcel

Key (in Bell)

C A B

From Area 1

Kali Statue

4

Artifact Piece

Postbox

Parcel

Palace of Evil

Indy and friends receive the warmest of welcomes upon reaching the palace, but it's all a big facade. As soon as dinner's over, they're assaulted by the palace's guards! Dispatch these brutes, then start smashing stuff in the dining hall for loot.

Nearly everything on the dinner table is smashable, all except for one odd block. Collect the block and place it near the mechanism on the wall as indicated.

Ring My Bell

Use Indy's whip to yank on the giant hanging bell to the right. A key falls out, but the noise attracts more guards! Deal with the guards, then take the key.

Use the key on the mechanism near the door to reveal a tiny alcove. Pull the alcove's lever to open the door so you may explore more of the palace.

Guards Galore

Many more guards attack you as you explore the palace's long halls. Defeat each enemy you encounter and smash everything you see in search of goodies.

Free Play Goodie
✊ 📗 Parcel 📦 ✊

This level's parcel sits atop a high ledge in the dining hall. You can only reach the parcel during Free Play mode. Have a super jump character leap from the barrel near the dining table to reach the high ledge above. Once there, toggle your character to Indy, then whip-swing over to the parcel.

You've got the parcel, but where's the postbox? Carry the parcel down the palace halls until you reach a Kali statue. Toggle to a character with the thuggee chant ability and then activate the statue to reveal the postbox. Drop the parcel inside, and off you go!

Indy's Bedroom

Enter the bedroom at the far end of the hall—the bedroom Indy would have slept in. Defeat the guards, then use Willie's scream ability to shatter the glass display case. Collect the blue book from within.

Exit Indy's bedroom and push the potted plant at the end of the hall. This causes the nearby shelf to slide away, revealing a hidden glyph puzzle! Use the blue book to solve the puzzle and open a secret passage leading into Willie's bedroom.

Willie's Bedroom

Defeat the guards that storm into Willie's bedroom through the main door, then shove her bed all the way over to the right. Use the nearby stool to get Indy to the top of the bed, then leap to the high whip point. Whip-swing over to the far ledge, then pull the lever you find there to drop some jiggling LEGO bits near the room's statue.

Stack the LEGO bits near the statue to add a handle to it. Push against the statue to grab its handle, then pull. The statue slides away from the wall, revealing a secret passage to the next area.

⚚ Artifact Piece 4 ⚚

Smash the potted plant in the alcove near the hallway's Kali statue to reveal a hidden artifact piece!

⚚ Artifact Piece 5 ⚚

Smash open one of the armoires in Indy's bedroom to discover an artifact piece tucked away inside.

⚚ Artifact Piece 6 ⚚

In Willie's Bedroom, slide the bed all the way over to the right. Then use Willie's superior jumping skill to leap up and grab the artifact piece that hovers high above.

Area 3: Secret Passage

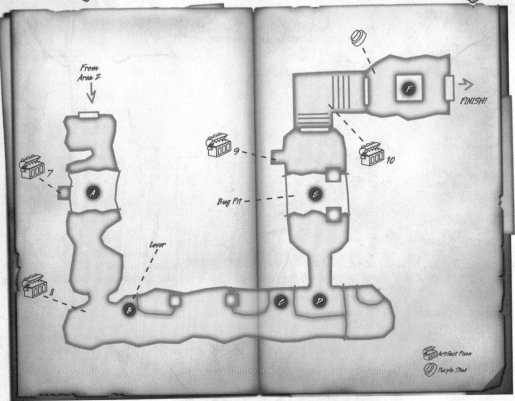

From Area 2

7

A

Lever

8

B

9

Bug Pit

E

10

C   D

FINISH!

F

Artifact Piece

Purple Stud

It's the Pits

A

There certainly is far more to this palace than meets the eye! There are many pits down the secret passage's first stretch, so be very careful as you go.

B

Pull the lever here to reveal a ladder. Climb up as Indy, then whip-swing across the wide gap that follows. Jump out and grab the vine that's dangling ahead, then switch to Short Round.

C

Stack the jiggling LEGO bits beneath Indy's vine to form a tiny door on the wall, then send Short Round crawling through. The little guy pops out from another door on a high ledge; jump to the left and grab hold of the dangling vine.

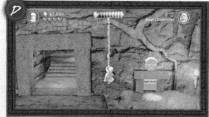
D

When both Indy and Short Round are hanging from the two vines, a large stone platform rises between them. Jump Indy and Short Round onto the platform. Willie uses the platform's handrails to reach the top.

It's Not Fortune Cookies...

E

Much to Willie's horror, the group encounters a bug-filled pit here. Whip-swing across as Indy, then snag a torch from the sconces near the door.

The bugs fear the fire. With torch in hand, cross the pit on foot and then lead your companions back across. Stand on the three buttons in front of the door beyond the bug pit to open it.

Terrible Trap

Use Indy's whip to yank on the loose brick that sticks out from the wall here, but beware. After you do, the ceiling begins to lower. You've sprung a deadly trap!

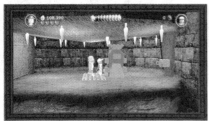

There's no time to lose. Destroy the two skeletons that fall from the ceiling to obtain two boxes of LEGO bits. Quickly place both boxes on the room's central green pad, then stack the bits to form a giant support pillar that halts the ceiling's descent. Level Complete!

🏺 Artifact Piece 7 🏺

While hanging from the secret passage's very first vine, jump to the right and land in the small nook to claim the artifact piece that sits within.

🏺 Artifact Piece 8 🏺

This one's hovering out in the open, just to the left of the doorway beyond the initial, pit-ridden stretch. Use Willie to grab it with ease.

🏺 Artifact Piece 9 🏺

After crossing the bug-filled pit, use Indy's whip to yank open a nook. Examine the nook; a skeleton drops down from above! Destroy the skeleton to obtain an artifact piece.

🏺 Artifact Piece 10 🏺

Smash the crates and vases beyond the bug pit to discover an artifact piece. It pays to destroy!

NOTE

Not too worry if the ceiling collapses. Your entire crew dies, but they all come back again. The trap resets itself though, so work fast and build that pillar!

TIP

Don't miss the purple stud in the booby trap room's corner.

THE TEMPLE OF KALI

Temple of Doom

It seems the humble villagers were right about Pankot Palace. Dr. Jones has discovered a secret passage within the palace walls—one that had led him to a massive underground temple filled with wicked cultists. As Indiana, Willie, and Short Round watch the men conduct some sort of bizarre ritual from afar, a cultist suddenly pops up behind them and steals Willie away! Indy and Short Round must now brave the temple to rescue Willie from a terrible fate.

STAGE COLLECTIBLES

Item	Area	Notes	Got It?
1	1	On high ledge near start (super jump ability required)	☐
2	1	Dig up 3 buried skulls (excavate ability required)	☐
3	1	On ledge near rotating platforms (explosion ability required)	☐
4	1	On low ledge near lava, beneath bridge	☐
5	1	In nook past bridge (steal turban; activate Kali statue)	☐
6	1	Atop first big rotating platform (climb to top)	☐
7	2	In high left nook (explosion and super jump abilities required)	☐
8	2	On left foreground ledge (repair ability required)	☐
9	2	In low left nook (collapse ledge to gain access)	☐
10	2	Atop giant Kali statue's head (climb up handrails)	☐
	2	In right foreground ledge's nook (academic and repair abilities required)	☐

True Adventurer stud requirement:
50,000 studs

Helpful Free Play Skills:

 Academic ability   Repair ability

Excavate ability   Super jump ability

Explosion ability

STORY MODE CHARACTERS

Indiana Jones   **Short Round**

Area 1: Lava Ledges

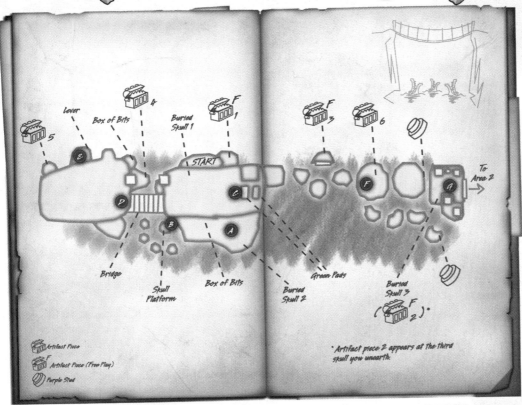

Artifact Piece

Artifact Piece (Free Play)

Purple Stud

* Artifact piece 2 appears at the third skull you unearth.

Evil Zealots

It's time to teach these rotten cultists a lesson! Drop down from the starting ledge and pummel the first group of enemies. Then run toward the foreground and drop off the ledge to defeat the cultists down below, at a lower ledge near the lava.

Stack the jiggling LEGO bits you discover at the lower ledge to build a short ladder. Climb up and then shove the giant statue out of the alcove so that it smashes on the ground.

Stack the statue's jiggling remains to build a spinner handle, then place the handle on the pole to the left to complete the spinner. Before using the spinner, first pick up the nearby box of LEGO bits and carry it onto the freaky skull platform here. Then switch to Short Round and push the green side of the spinner's handle to raise the skull platform like an elevator.

Switch back to Indy and place the box of bits on one of the two green pads here, in front of a large statue. One more box to find!

Raise the Bridge, Get the Bits

Whip-swing across the gap to the left and dispatch the large group of cultists that attacks you. Next, take two torches from the nearby sconces and use them to light the torches of the lowered bridge. The bridge rises when both torches are lit, and Short Round dashes across to join you.

TIP

One of the cultists beyond the bridge is painted white. After you defeat him, try to snatch this high-ranking acolyte's hat (a black turban) for future use!

Switch to Short Round and slip through the tiny door beyond the bridge to reach the lever in this high ledge. Pull the lever, then crawl back through the tiny door. The ground in front of the first tiny door has risen—collect the box of bits from the high ledge you're now able to reach.

Place the second box of bits on the other green pad in front of the large statue, then stack the jiggling bits to give the statue a flat top and some handrails. Use the handrails to reach the top of the statue, then leap to the nearby ledge.

Free Play Goodies

🏆 Artifact Piece 1 🏆

Revisit this level in Free Play mode and use a character who has the super jump ability (any female character) to reach the artifact piece on the high ledge right near the start. Just jump up and grab it!

⚔ Artifact Piece 2 ⚔

Use a character with the excavate ability to dig up three skulls in this area. (Check the map for their locations.) After digging up the third skull, you're awarded an artifact piece!

Free Play Goodies (Continued)

🏆 Artifact Piece 3 🏆

Use a character with the explosion ability to blast the silver pipes covering up the ledge near the huge rotating platforms. Now leap to the ledge to nab an artifact piece.

Crossing the Cavern

Hop along ledges and swing from ropes to reach a pair of massive rotating platforms to the right. The platforms are covered in handrails; jump from the first rotating platform to the second, then onto the far right ledge.

Once both characters have navigated the rotating platforms and reached the far ledge, pull one of the levers near the door. Your partner follows suit and the door opens. Dash through to reach the next area when you're ready to move on.

TIP

Step on the floor switches to open the chests near the area's exit door and score some extra studs. Also, don't miss the purple stud near the second rotating platform, or the other one on the platform way down near the lava below!

🏆 Artifact Piece 4 🏆

Hop across the small rocks that float on the lava near the skull platform to reach a background ledge that sports an artifact piece. Easy grab!

🏆 Artifact Piece 5 🏆

If you managed to swipe the acolyte's turban, you can fool the Kali statue beyond the bridge into thinking you're a cult member! Pray at the statue to raise the nearby gate and gain access to the artifact piece in the nook beyond. Claiming the turban can be tough, though—if you missed it, make things easier by revisiting this level in Free Play mode and using a character who has the thuggee chant ability to activate the Kali statue with less fuss.

🏆 Artifact Piece 6 🏆

Climb to the top of the first giant rotating platform to claim an artifact piece you discover up there. This can be done without a super jump character if you leap between the two rotating platforms, working your way steadily upward.

Area 2: Sacrificial Pit

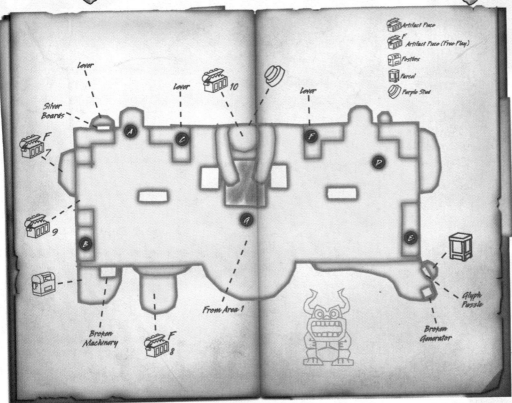

Artifact Piece

F Artifact Piece (Free Play)

Posties

Parcel

Purple Stud

Lever

Silver Boards

F 7

9

B

From Area 1

Broken Machinery

F 8

Lever

Lever

10

Lever

F

D

E

Glyph Puzzle

Broken Generator

Den of Evil

Oh, no! The cultists are lowering Willie into some sort of devious sacrificial pit. You've got to save her! Smash the wooden boards here to access a key mechanism in a small nook. Turn the key to cause a nearby statue to slide away from the wall.

Climb the ladder here to reach the ledge above. Much of the ledge collapses when you reach the top—whip-swing across to the far side, then leap across the statue you pulled out from the wall.

Yank the lever on the ledge near the giant Kali statue to raise Willie's cage up from the lava pit. The cage doesn't rise all the way—there's one more lever to pull!

Sliding Statues

Stack the large pile of jiggling LEGO bits here to complete the nearby statue. Slide the statue along its checker-floor track, positioning it against the far right wall. Pull the other nearby statue out of the recess in the background wall for future use.

Free Play Goodies

Artifact Piece 7

Blast the silver pipes in the area's upper-left corner to gain access to a lever in a nook. Pull the lever to extend a series of platforms from the left wall.

Switch to a female character and super-jump along the platforms to reach a high ledge way up near the ceiling. Claim the artifact piece you discover up here.

Continued on next page

Free Play Goodies (continued)

Artifact Piece 8

Use a character with the repair ability to fix the broken machinery sitting on the area's left foreground ledge. This raises a platform from the lava, revealing a secret artifact piece!

Parcel

Fix the generator sitting on the right foreground ledge to gain access to a glyph puzzle. Toggle to a character who has the academic ability to solve the puzzle and obtain this level's parcel from the nook beyond.

Carry the parcel across the cavern and onto the left foreground ledge. Smash the little shrine here to reveal some jiggling LEGO bits, then stack those bits to build a postbox. Drop your parcel in the postbox to mail it back to Barnett College.

Saving Willie

Smash the odd little shrine here to reveal a tiny door, then send Short Round crawling through to reach the ledge above.

Hop across the statues you've positioned to reach another lever near the giant Kali statue. Pull this second lever to raise Willie even farther out of the pit.

Showdown: Chatter Lal

Willie's now out of immediate danger, but you're not! Chatter Lal comes barging into the area, dressed in full cultist garb. Punch the madman until he leaps onto one of the two red vents to either side of the central lava pit.

Chatter Lal flees whenever you approach him from this point forward, leaping between the two red vents. To harm him, defeat one of the white-skinned acolyte enemies, then take his hat (a black turban) to disguise yourself as a cultist.

After you've acquired a turban, chant at one of the two smaller Kali statues that stand at either side of the giant Kali statue. After you do so, hot rocks and lava begin to spout up from the red vents! Keep chanting and chasing Chatter Lal about, steering him into the lava spouts until you finally manage to sear the evil out of him. Level complete!

Artifact Piece 9

After climbing the ladder and collapsing the weak ledge, drop to the ground and nab an artifact piece from the small nook you can now enter.

Artifact Piece 10

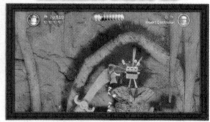

Jump to one of the giant Kali statue's arms and then climb up the statue's handrails to reach the artifact piece that sits atop its head. Don't miss the purple stud up here, either!

FREE THE SLAVES

For the Children

Indiana has saved Willie from the cultists' evil grip. Now he must save the many innocent children the cult has kidnapped! These zealots have been stealing young people from nearby villages and forcing them to work in their mining tunnels as slaves. It's time to put an end to this horrible treatment and return the kids to their families!

STAGE COLLECTIBLES

Item	Area	Notes	Got It?
1	1	On high ledge near lava (tiny size ability required)	☐
2	1	On high ledge above Kali statue (thuggee chant ability required)	☐
3	1	On high platform beyond lava (use Indy's whip to reach)	☐
4	2	On low ledge beneath wooden platforms	☐
5	2	On high platform near area exit (use lift to reach)	☐
6	3	Chant at Kali statue to reveal (thuggee chant ability required)	☐
7	3	On high ledge (tiny size ability required)	☐
8	3	Bring cog to engine, then fix with wrench to reveal	☐
9	4	Climb to high ledge with Short Round and collect	☐
10	4	Dig up three buried skulls to get	☐
	2	In nook near trolly (blow up silver boards; explosion ability required)	☐

True Adventurer stud requirement: 65,000 studs

Helpful Free Play Skills:

- Explosion ability
- Thuggee chant ability
- Tiny size ability

STORY MODE CHARACTERS

Indiana Jones (Kali)

Willie

Area 1: Mining Tunnel

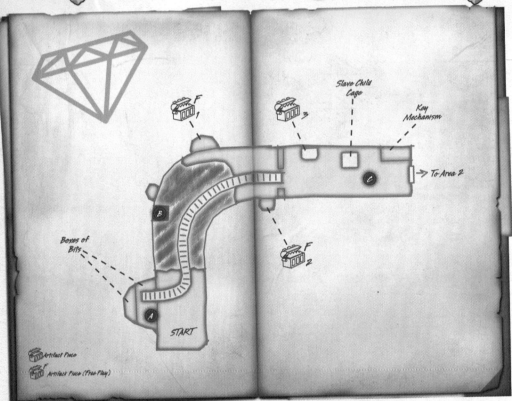

F1

3

Slave Child Cage

Key Mechanism

→ To Area 2

C

B

Boxes of Bits

F2

A

START

Artifact Piece

Artifact Piece (Free Play)

No More Short Round

Willie's back at Indy's side, but now the cultists have kidnapped Short Round! Switch to Willie and leap onto the high ledge near the starting point. Then stack the nearby jiggling bits to build a handrail so that Indy can climb up as well.

Find a box of LEGO bits on the ledge and place it onto one of the two green pads. Stack the jiggling bits to add a lever to the nearby mine rail.

Use Indy's whip at the ledge's whip point to tug on an overhead switch. This raises a nearby platform. Switch to Willie and use the platform to reach the high ledge above, where you discover a second box of LEGO bits.

Place the second box of bits on the other green pad, then stack the jiggling bits to add a second lever to the mine rail. When both levers are in place, the rail is lifted, and its cart is sent zipping on ahead. The cart crashes into a distant wooden wall, opening a way forward!

Free Play Goodies
Artifact Piece 1

Revisit this level in Free Play mode and use a tiny character to crawl through the little door in the nook near the lava. You emerge from another door on a high ledge, right next to an artifact piece!

Continued on next page

Free Play Goodies (continued)

👐 🤖 Artifact Piece 2 🤖 👐

Chant at the Kali statue across the lava pit with a Free Play character who has the thuggee chant ability. The statue then shatters, revealing a steamy updraft! Step into the draft to float up and collect the artifact piece from the ledge above.

Crossing the Lava

Use rope and handrail to cross the lava pit here, then wipe out the cultists that attack you on the far side.

The First Slave Child

Leap onto the low platform at the far end of the tunnel, then turn the key mechanism.

This lowers a hanging cage, releasing an imprisoned slave child! Grateful, the little kid crawls through a nearby tiny door to reach a high ledge, then pulls a lever for you to open the nearby door. Thanks, kid!

🤖 Artifact Piece 3 🤖

Use Indy's whip at the whip point beyond the lava pit to yank down some LEGO bits from the platform above. Stack the bits to create a handrail, then use the handrail to reach the artifact piece that sits atop the ledge.

Area 2: Cavern

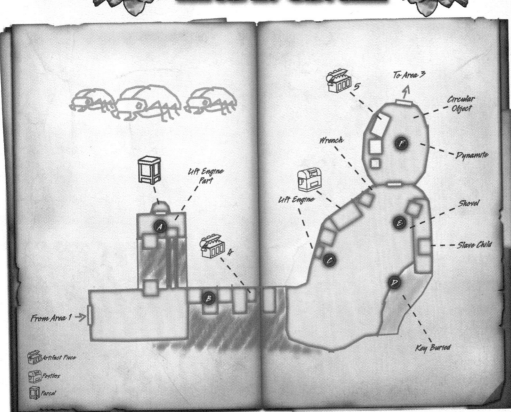

Whip It Good

Use Indy's whip to cross over to this ledge. Smash a crate to find an object you need, then place the object on the green trolly. Turn the nearby key to roll the trolly across the pit, dumping the object on the ledge near Willie.

Indy's whip is the only way to bring the object across the wooden platforms to the right. Jump to the first wooden platform, then turn around and snatch the object with Indy's whip. Now drop the object and jump to the next platform ahead. Use the whip to snag the object once more. Repeat this until you manage to cross the wooden ledges with the object.

Fixing the Lift

Place the object on the lift engine here, then smash some nearby crates and barrels to find a wrench. Use the wrench to repair the lift engine and activate the lift.

Before riding the lift, smash apart the junk on the cavern's right side to discover a shovel and an odd circular object. Take the shovel and use it to dig up a key that's buried in the nearby pool of water.

Insert the key into the nearby mechanism and turn it to raise a whip point for Indy. Now ride the lift and swing from the whip point to reach the top of the far-right platform.

Free Play Goodie

📦 Parcel 📦

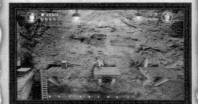

Use a character with the explosion ability to destroy the silver boards near the trolly. Collect the parcel you discover in the nook beyond, then use the trolly to ferry the parcel across the lava pit.

Use Indy's whip to get the parcel across the wooden platforms, just as you did with the lift engine part. Then simply ride the lift and deposit the parcel into the postbox on the ledge above, sending it back to Barnett College.

The Second Slave Child

Punch the door of the cage you find atop the far-right platform to free another slave child. The kid quickly scurries through a tiny door to reach a high ledge, then pulls a

lever. This opens the door ahead, allowing you to explore more of the cavern.

Dispatch the host of cultists that attacks you here, then collect some dynamite from a nearby crate. Hurl the dynamite at the silver wreckage ahead to clear the way forward.

🏆 Artifact Piece 4 🏆

This one's all too easy: Explore the skinny ledge below the stretch of wooden platforms to find an artifact piece sitting at the far end.

🏆 Artifact Piece 5 🏆

Smash the crates and barrels near the box of dyamite to discover a strange circular object. Place this object on the green pad near the lift. This forms a button on the ground.

Step on the button with one character to lower the nearby lift. Switch to the other character and board the lift, then switch characters again and move off the button. The lift then rises. Switch characters once more and collect the artifact piece from the high platform.

Area 3: Slave Pen

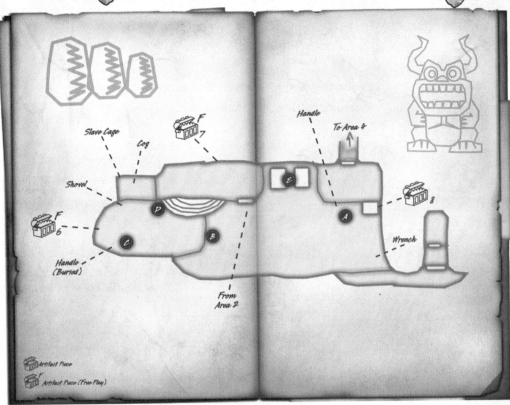

More Slaves to Save

Indy and Willie have finally reached the heart of the temple's cavernous mining facility. Smash the debris here to discover a handle, then carry the handle to the left.

Affix the handle to the green notch that sticks out from the wall here. Push against the handle to grab it, then pull to yank out a series of steps leading up to the ledge above.

Freeing the Slaves

Pummel the cultists on the ledge, then smash a nearby shelf to obtain a shovel. Use the shovel to dig up another handle from the nearby patch of shimmering soil.

TIP

Keep hold of a shovel for future use in the next area.

Attach the handle to the green notch on the wall near the cage full of slave children, then pull the handle to open the cage. The remainder of the children that had been captured by the cult leap out and sprint to safety. Great work!

Free Play Goodies

Artifact Piece 6

Revisit this area with a character who has the thuggee chant ability, then chant at the Kali statue near the slave cage. The Kali statue then explodes, revealing a hidden artifact piece!

Artifact Piece 7

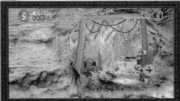

Use a character who's tiny to crawl through the little door near the slave cage. This takes you to a high, overhead ledge, where you discover an artifact piece.

Little Help

Instead of fleeing, one of the slave children uses a nearby tiny door to reach a high ledge. The child then pulls a lever for you, raising some platforms to the right so you may continue exploring the mines. Leap across the platforms to reach the far ledge, then wail away at the debris to clear the path to the next area.

Artifact Piece 8

After freeing the slaves, switch to Willie and leap into the slave cage. Smash the debris to find a cog, then carry the cog to the engine near the area's far-right side.

Place the cog on the engine, then smash the nearby crates to discover a wrench. Use the wrench to repair the engine, which then starts up, runs for a moment, and then explodes into an artifact piece!

Area 4: Rock Crusher

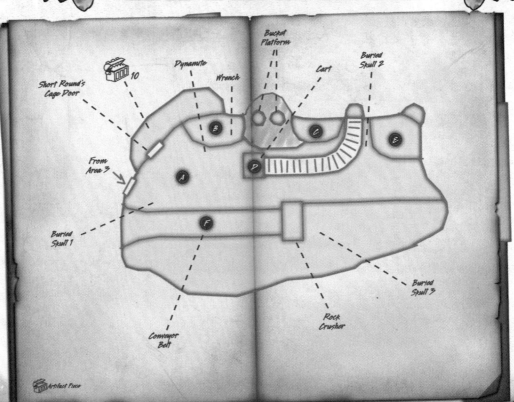

Short Round's Cage Door

From Area 3

Buried Skull 1

Dynamite

Wrench

Bucket Platform

Cart

Buried Skull 2

Conveyor Belt

Rock Crusher

Buried Skull 3

Artifact Piece

A Friend in Need

Indy and Willie discover Short Round trapped inside a cage in this final area. Unfortunately, a burly slave driver isn't about to let the trio leave without a fight! Take a few swings at the slave driver until you knock him out.

Indy's fists make short work of the evil slave driver, but the fight doesn't end there. The Maharaja himself soon appears on a high ledge and tosses some sort of devious smoke bomb at the unconscious brute. The potent fumes awaken the slave driver, bringing him back to full health!

Indy's unable to defeat the slave driver while the Maharaja keeps interfering. Quickly collect some dynamite from the nearby crate and hurl the dynamite at the silver bars of Short Round's cage to free him. Then take control of Short Round and crawl through the nearby tiny door.

Messin' with the Maharaja

Short Round pops out of a tiny door on the Maharaja's ledge. Punch the wicked boy-prince a few times to make him flee, then smash the nearby objects to find a wrench. Use the wrench to repair the hanging bucket to the right so that it starts moving up and down like an elevator.

Keep control of Short Round and cross the hanging buckets to reach the next ledge ahead. Pummel the Maharaja here on this ledge to make him flee once more.

A Helping Hand

Short Round needs help getting over to the Maharaja's final ledge. Switch to Indy or Willie and shove the large cart along its track as far as it will go. Then switch back to Short Round and use the cart as a platform to help you reach the far ledge.

Punch the Maharaja a few more times until you finally manage to snap him out of his stupor. The young prince is grateful, but the slave driver must still be defeated!

Showdown: Slave Driver

The slave driver flees to the nearby conveyer belt and begins hurling giant boulders at you. You can't reach the man to punch him, but you can throw dynamite at him from afar! Dodge his boulders and toss explosives at the slave driver until you defeat him. Level complete!

⚙ Artifact Piece 9 ⚙

If you kept a shovel from the previous area, use it to dig up three buried skulls in the ground about the rock crusher area. (Check the map for their locations.) Unearth all three skulls and you're awarded an artifact piece for your effort! Of course, you can always revisit this level in Free Play mode with a character who has the excavate ability to make digging up the skulls a little easier.

⚙ Artifact Piece 10 ⚙

After freeing Short Round and chasing off the Maharaja for the first time, have the little guy jump up and grab onto some overhead handrails. Use the handrails to reach a high ledge, where an artifact piece awaits discovery.

ESCAPE THE MINES

A Ride to Remember

Dr. Jones has managed to free the children enslaved by the cult. Now he, Willie, and Short Round must make a daring escape from the mines! Cultists are everywhere, determined not to let the trio flee. Running low on options, Indiana sees no other choice but to escape the mines by mine cart.

STAGE COLLECTIBLES

Item	Area	Notes	Got It?
1	1	On Kali statue ledge (thuggee chant ability required)	☐
2	1	On low foreground ledge (drop off cliff near ladder)	☐
3	1	Above ledge near mine cart (use Willie to reach)	☐
4	1	In nook left of cart rail lift (use Willie to reach)	☐
5	2	Sitting out in the open just off the track (lean to get)	☐
6	2	Derail 3 enemy mine carts to get	☐
7	2	Whack 3 overhead devices to get	☐
8	3	Sitting out in the open just off the track (lean to get)	☐
9	3	Derail 3 enemy mine carts to get	☐
10	3	Whack 3 overhead devices to get	☐
	1	Solve glyph puzzle and excavate (academic and excavate abilites required)	☐

True Adventurer stud requirement: 120,000 studs

Helpful Free Play Skills:

Academic ability

Excavate ability

Thuggee chant ability

STORY MODE CHARACTERS

Indiana Jones (Kali)

Willie (Ceremony Dress)

Short Round

Area 1: Cart Depot

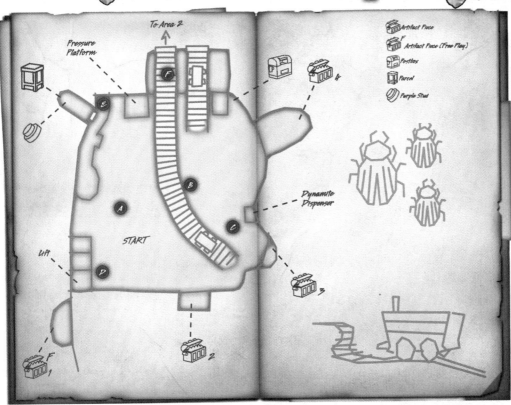

To Area 2

Pressure
Platform

F

E

B

A

START

Lift

D

F
1

2

Dynamite
Dispenser

3

4

Artifact Piece

Artifact Piece (Free Play)

Postbox

Parcel

Purple Stud

Repairing the Cart Rail

You must repair the mine cart and rail before making your escape. Beat up the many cultists who attack you first, then find a large piece of cart rail on the ground here. Collect the cart rail and place it on the track where indicated.

Step across the track and smash the crates near the wrench. Collect the wrench, then stack the jiggling LEGO bits left by the crates to complete the track.

Fixing the Mine Cart

Pull the lever on the wall here to make the nearby machine dispense some dynamite. Hurl the dynamite at the pile of rubble to the right, then stack the jiggling bits that remain to rebuild the mine cart.

With the mine cart fully assembled, use the wrench you found near the track to repair it. Then push the cart along the track as far as it will go.

Free Play Goodies
Artifact Piece 1

Send Short Round crawling through the tiny door near the lift. He pops out of another door on a distant ledge. Once there, toggle your Free Play character to one that has the thuggee chant ability, then activate the Kali statue to reveal a secret artifact piece!

Continued on next page

Free Play Goodies (continued)
🗃 Parcel 🗃

During Free Play mode, solve the glyph puzzle on the left wall to reveal a small secret passage. Enter the passage to nab a purple stud, then toggle to a character with the excavate ability.

Dig at the passage's sparkling mound to unearth this level's parcel. Score! The postbox is near the cart rail lift. Carry the parcel over and drop it in the chute to mail it back to Barnett College.

Raising the Rail

Now you just need to raise the rail. Position Indy on the lift here, then switch to another character and turn the nearby key. The lift rises, allowing Indy to traverse the ledges ahead.

Pull the lever on the wall here to lower a ladder, then jump onto the platform to the right. The platform sinks a bit, and the cart rail rises. Remain on the platform until Willie and Short Round climb up the ladder and join Indy, adding their weight to the platform. This fully raises the cart rail and locks it in place.

Off We Go!

With the mine cart raised, all that's left to do is shove it forward. The gate ahead opens and the crazy cart ride begins!

🗃 Artifact Piece 2 🗃

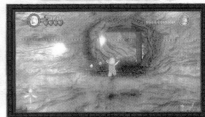

Run to the foreground and spy a ladder leading down the cliff. Drop off the cliff to land on a tiny ledge below the ladder, where an artifact piece is hidden.

🗃 Artifact Piece 3 🗃

Switch to Willie and jump on top of the barricade at the mine track's far-right end. From there, leap to the top of the ledge above.

Once atop the ledge, jump up and grab the overhead handrail. Then leap up to collect the artifact piece hovering high above.

🗃 Artifact Piece 4 🗃

This one's an easy find. Use Willie's awesome jumping skill to reach a high nook to the right of the cart rail lift. An artifact piece awaits collection up there.

Area 2: Cart Rail A

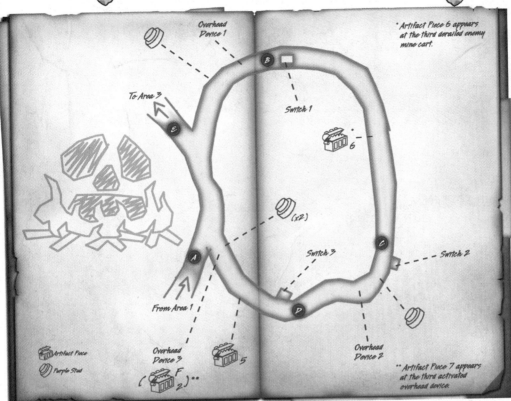

Overhead Device 1

* Artifact Piece 6 appears at the third derailed enemy mine cart.

To Area 3

Switch 1

E

6

(x2)

Switch 3

C

Switch 2

A

From Area 1

D

Artifact Piece

Purple Stud

Overhead Device 3

5

Overhead Device 2

(F 2)**

** Artifact Piece 7 appears at the third activated overhead device.

Hold onto Your Fedora!

Push left or right to lean the cart. You need to do this to hit some targets.

The mine carts take off at tremendous speed, with Indy in the left cart, and Willie and Short Round in the one on the right. Your escape has begun!

Hit the signals to line up the tracks and escape the mines.

The mine carts follow an endless loop around the rail until you manage to activate three switches. The first switch is located here; lean over and whack the switch with a shovel to trigger it. Since the switch is in the middle of the track, any character can hit it.

TIP

Onscreen indicators appear to inform you when a switch is coming up and which cart to use. Pay attention!

TIP

Many purple studs can be nabbed along the cart rail. Lean to collect these special prizes. Refer to the map for their locations. You can also smash hanging lanterns for silver and gold studs if you like.

The second switch is just ahead, on the left. Have Indy lean over and whack it as his cart speeds past.

Shifting the Track

The third and final switch can only be reached by Willie and Short Round. When you're ready to leave this area, have them lean to the right and smack it.

When all three switches have been activated, the track shifts, sending our heros through a different tunnel and into the unknown.

NOTE

Each time you hit a switch, one of the icons at the top of the screen lights up. The switches deactivate after awhile, as indicated by their icons. (If you keep missing one, others you've hit will eventually deactivate.) All three switches must be activated in order to shift the track and advance.

Artifact Piece 6

While zipping along the track, whack three enemy mine carts with your shovel to knock them off the rails. After you derail your third enemy cart, you're awarded an artifact piece.

Artifact Piece 5

Indy must lean left to nab this artifact piece, which is located just a few feet beyond the third and final switch.

Artifact Piece 7

Pan your camera view upward and notice the strange devices above the track. Whack all three of these overhead devices to obtain a secret artifact piece! You don't need to lean to hit these objects; just swing away with the shovel. Check the map to see the devices' locations.

Area 3: Cart Rail B

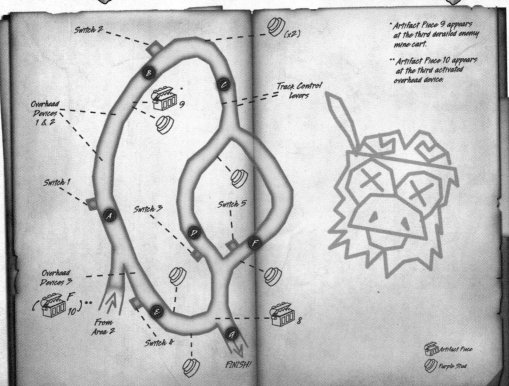

* Artifact Piece 9 appears at the third derailed enemy mine cart.

** Artifact Piece 10 appears at the third activated overhead device.

Keep On Carting

The second mine cart rail is much like the first, only longer and with five switches for you to activate. The first switch is here; Indy must lean out to whack it.

Keep control of Indy and whack the second switch here.

A Fork in the Rail

The levers here control your path of travel at the fork in the track ahead. By default, you are set to travel down the right rail. But if you have Indy smack the lever on his side, you will travel down the left stretch of track instead. You'll eventually need to venture down both stretches, as there's a switch to hit near the end of each. Leave the levers be at first and continue down the right rail.

Have Willie and Short Round whack the third switch at the right rail's end (just before you merge back with the main track).

Indy must be the one to hit the fourth switch here.

Take the Left Tunnel!

On your second lap, have Indy whack the track control lever on his side of the rail. This causes your cart to zip down the left rail. Don't miss the track control lever or you'll have to start all over again!

Hit the fifth and final switch here, at the end of the fork's left rail (just before you merge back with the main track). Don't miss it!

With all five switches activated, the track shifts beyond the fork, sending our heroes down a different track and putting and end to the harrowing cart ride. Level complete!

TIP

If the switches keep deactivating on you in this final area, just ride the rail and collect goodies until they all revert to a deactivated state. Then do your best to hit them all in two laps, making sure to switch the track at the fork during your second lap so you can hit the switch down the other stretch.

Artifact Piece 8

This artifact piece sits right out in the open along the track. Have Indy lean out and collect this prize.

Artifact Piece 9

Derail three enemy mine carts in the cart rail B area to win an artifact piece prize. You'll need to explore the entire rail to find all three enemy carts, as there's one to derail along each stretch of track beyond the fork. Start swinging as soon as you see them; it takes a few hits to get the job done!

Artifact Piece 10

While speeding along the second mine rail, pan your camera view upward and notice the strange devices above the track. Whack all three of these overhead devices to obtain a secret artifact piece, just as you did at the first mine rail area. You don't need to lean to hit these objects; just swing away with the shovel. Check the map to see their locations.

BATTLE ON THE BRIDGE

An Epic Clash

Desperate times call for desperate measures, and Indy, Short Round, and Willie have somehow managed to overcome the odds and survive a dramatic cart ride through the mines. The trio hopes they've outrun their pursuers, but the cultists haven't given up! Now they've dumped a massive tank of water into the mine tunnels, aiming to drown the three intruders. The drama continues!

STAGE COLLECTIBLES

Item	Area	Notes	Got It?
F₁	1	In nook near level start (explosion ability required)	☐
2	1	At far end of water tunnel (must outrun the water)	☐
F₃	2	Buried in caged-off cave (excavation ability required)	☐
4	2	On lowest ledge to the right of the waterfall	☐
F₅	3	On high ledge (solve glyph puzzle; academic ability required)	☐
6	3	In fifth leaf-covered pit	☐
7	3	Hidden behind boulder beyond leaf-covered pits	☐
8	3	Dig up vase and place on central pressure plate to reveal	☐
9	4	Sitting atop farthest circular platform toward foreground	☐
10	4	In grass beyond bridge (make smiley face out of flowers)	☐
	4	In secret cave beyond bridge (explosion ability required)	☐

True Adventurer stud requirement: 80,000 studs

Helpful Free Play Skills:

Academic ability

Excavate ability

Explosion ability

STORY MODE CHARACTERS

Indiana Jones (Kali)   **Willie (Ceremony)**   **Short Round**

Area 1: Water Chase

Pitfalls and Manholes

Water will burst out from the manhole covers in the tunnel. Avoid these potential hazards as you rush to outrun the main cascade.

There's a small circular platform in the middle of this second wide pit. Hop across the platform to cross the pit safely.

Tricky Bridge

You're close to the end when you reach this narrow bridge, but beware: There are a few tiny pits just past the bridge, and it's tough to see them. Look for the pits as you cross the bridge and do your best to jump them!

Artifact Piece 2

Reach the end of the tunnel ahead of the rushing water to claim the artifact piece that sits at the tunnel's far end. Nice run!

Water! Water! ... WATER!!!

Be careful what you wish for, Indy! Immediately dash toward the foreground when the action begins, sprinting down the tunnel and keeping ahead of the rushing torrent behind you.

As with the Lost Temple's boulder chase scenario, you'll earn a nice prize if you manage to reach the end of this area without being flushed away.

Free Play Goodie
Artifact Piece 1

Revisit this level in Free Play mode and choose a character that has the explosion ability to be your main character. Quickly destroy the silver boards near the start point, then dash into the alcove beyond to collect a hidden artifact piece. Speed is key; it doesn't take long for the rushing water to wash you away!

Area 2: Cliffs of Insanity

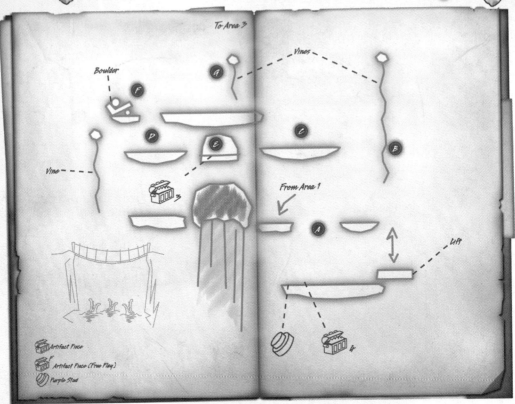

Artifact Piece
Artifact Piece (Free Play)
Purple Stud

Cliff-Hangers

That was close! Indy finds himself standing on a ledge to one side of the waterfall; Willie and Short Round are across the way. Keep control of Indy and whip-swing across this gap to reach the next ledge.

Jump and grab onto the dangling vine here, then climb to the top. Jump from the top of the vine, aiming to grab the handrail of the ledge below and to the left.

Indy has gone as far has he can for now. Leave him standing on this ledge and switch over to Short Round.

Bridging the Gap

As Short Round, jump up and climb the nearby vine to reach the ledge above. Crawl through the tiny door you discover up here.

Short Round emerges from another small door in a cave sealed by bars. Collect the key and return through the door.

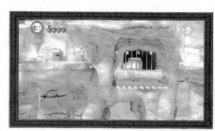

Use the key at the mechanism near the first tiny door to extend a wooden bridge. Now Indy can cross over and join his friends.

PRIMA OFFICIAL GAME GUIDE

Free Play Goodie

⛏ 👑 Artifact Piece 3 👑 ⛏

An artifact piece is buried in the key cave. Return here during Free Play mode and toggle Short Round to a character with the excavate ability to dig it up.

Movin' On Up

With the trio reunited, switch to Indy and use his whip to tug down an overhead boulder. Stack the jiggling LEGO bits the boulder leaves behind to form some handrails leading upward.

Climb the handrails you've built to reach an overhead ledge, then climb this rope. Jump to the nearby handrail and climb onto the top of the cliff. Whew! Run into the background to reach the next area.

👑 Artifact Piece 4 👑

You most likely didn't miss this artifact piece, which sits on the ledge below Indy's starting point. Drop down to collect it, then use the nearby lift to return to the ledges above.

Area 3: Mountain Path

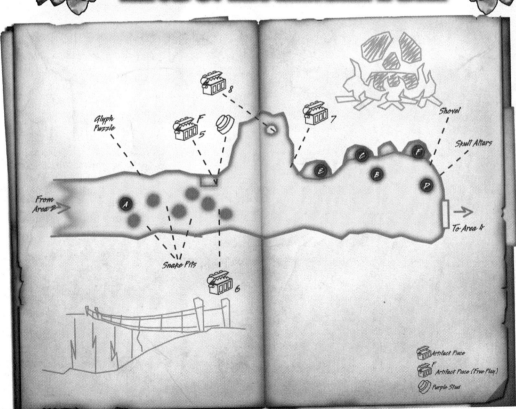

Path of Hazards

Use care when dashing along this rocky path. Those piles of leaves are actually covering pits full of deadly spikes!

Defeat the cultists that attack you as you advance along the trail. Use Indy's whip to yank down the ladder here, but don't climb up just yet.

Free Play Goodie

Artifact Piece 5

During Free Play mode, toggle your character to one who has the academic ability, then solve the glyph puzzle on the wall near the spike pits. This causes some stones to rise out of the ground. Hop up them to reach a high ledge with an artifact piece.

Sacred Stones

To open the gate to the right, Indy and pals must acquire three sacred stones. Defeat the next group of cultists that appears to attack you, then hurry to outfit Indy with the turban dropped by the cultist in white. After

donning the turban, climb up the ladder you pulled down earlier.

Indy discovers a strange statue on the ledge atop the ladder. His disguise allows Indy to perform the thuggee chant ability, activating the Kali statue and revealing a blue sacred stone that was hidden in the ledge!

Insert the blue sacred stone into the blue skull altar here as indicated. The alter lowers a bit, as does the nearby gate.

Willie's Stone

Defeat the next group of cultists, and this time, let Willie take their leader's turban. Then use Willie's exceptional jumping ability to reach the Kali statue atop this high ledge. Perform the thuggee chant to appease the statue and obtain another sacred stone. Place the stone as you did before to lower the gate a bit more.

Short Round's Stone

Find a shovel leaning against the wall at the trail's far end and use it to dig up an odd statue head from the ground nearby. Smash the statue head afterward to reduce it to jiggling bits, then stack those bits to form a tiny door on the wall.

As before, outfit Short Round with the thuggee turban, then send him crawling through the tiny door you've built. This allows Short Round to reach a third Kali statue. Pray at the statue to acquire the last sacred stone, then place it into the appropriate altar slot. The gate opens fully. Hurry through to the next area.

Artifact Piece 6

You want to avoid those leaf-covered pitfalls—all except one, that is! Going left to right, drop into the fifth leaf-covered pit you encounter to discover a hidden artifact piece. What a nice surprise!

Artifact Piece 7

Beyond the leaf-covered spike pits, stop to search behind a large rock and claim the artifact piece you can see shining out from behind it.

Artifact Piece 8

After obtaining the shovel at the trail's far end, use it to dig up a vase from the sparkling soil near the middle of the area. Place the vase on the nearby pad to fill it with flowers and obtain a secret artifact piece!

Area 4: The Gorge

Artifact Piece
Postbox
Parcel
Purple Stud

From Area 3

To Area 5

Wooden Lookout

Simply Gorgeous

Has Indy reached a dead end? No! Pan your camera view downward to spy a small, circular ledge ahead, then leap across.

TIP

Use character shadows to help you gauge your landings during each jump.

Use Indy's whip at the whip point here to pull down a portion of the wooden lookout ahead. Backtrack around to reach the lookout, which you're now able to climb atop.

Lowering the Bridge

Whip-swing over to this ledge, then smash the nearby boulder to loosen the bridge. One more boulder to smash!

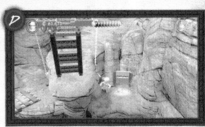

Switch to Short Round and leap to the far-right ledge, which features a tiny door. Crawl through to reach another ledge near the bridge. Destroy the boulder there, and the bridge comes crashing down.

Free Play Goodie

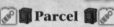 Parcel

After crossing the bridge, look for some weeds that are covering a hole to the right. Destroy the weeds to uncover the hole, then drop down to visit a secret cave.

Toggle your Free Play character to one with the explosion ability, then blow up the cave's metal blocks. This reveals a secret nook, where another box of LEGO bits is hidden. Take the sword and place the bits on the nearby green pad.

Use the shovel you acquired in the previous area to dig up this level's parcel from the cave floor. Now you just need to find the postbox!

Toss the sword at the overhead rope to bring down another box of bits in a small cage. Place this second box of bits on the green pad as well, then stack the jiggling LEGO bits to build the postbox. Now you can mail the parcel back to Barnett College!

The Final Gate

Indy, Willie, and Short Round must work together to open the final gate beyond the bridge. Destroy the weeds near the wall here to discover a tiny door, then send Short Round crawling through. The little guy pops out from another door on a high ledge.

Guide Short Round across the handrails near the ledge, then jump and grab the rope that hangs near the gate. Leave Short Round hanging on the rope and switch to Willie.

Only Willie has the grace to jump up and grab hold of the other rope that hangs near the gate. Leave her hanging on the rope, then switch to Indy.

Short Round and Willie are hanging from the gate's ropes. A skull-shaped pressure plate rises in front of the gate. Have Indy step onto this gruesome trigger to open the way forward. The final battle is at hand!

Artifact Piece 9

Keep leaping toward the foreground as you cross the gorge's initial stretch of circular ledges. The farthest ledge sports an artifact piece!

Artifact Piece 10

Run through the grass in the left nook beyond the bridge, and notice that flowers begin to sprout. Quickly dash about the grass to form a smiley face pattern with the flowers before they shrink away. Once you complete the face (two eyes and a mouth), an artifact piece appears as the nose! Collect this worthy prize.

Area 5: Bridge Battle

Showdown: Mola Ram

The gang faces the final battle against Mola Ram and his fanatical followers on a treacherous rope bridge. Defeat the cultists that rush forward to attack you, and wait for Mola Ram himself to attack Indy. Fight back until the cult leader paralyzes Indy, then quickly switch to Willie or Short Round and hit the evil man to wound him and drive him off.

Mola Ram flees after you hurt him, and more cultists rush in to attack. Some of the men now carry swords; obtain a sword and toss it at one of the bridge's four anchor pins to destroy it.

TIP

Make sure you're targeting the anchor pins before you throw your sword. Look for the blue arrows.

Mola Ram returns after you destory the anchor pin. Hurt him again while he paralyzes Indy to drive him off, then claim a sword and toss it at another anchor pin. Repeat this process to destroy all four anchor pins and collapse the bridge. Story complete! Sit back and enjoy the ending.

THE HUNT FOR SIR RICHARD

A Heroic Adventure

Dr. Jones has been on many journeys in search of fortune and glory. This time, however, Indy's goal is much nobler: His father, Henry Jones Sr., has gone missing, and it's up to Indy to find him! Indy's dad was last seen in the city of Venice, Italy, where he was searching for clues to the whereabouts of the Holy Grail. Indiana and his friend, Marcus Brody, waste no time in hopping a plane to Venice. Arriving there, the two meet up with Dr. Elsa Schnider—a beautiful young woman who had been assisting Indy's father up to the moment when he disappeared. The search begins....

STAGE COLLECTIBLES

Item	Area	Notes	Got It?
F1	1	In balcony window (glass-shattering ability required)	☐
F2	1	Atop high patio, to the left (tiny size ability required)	☐
F3	1	Drive moped into cones to reveal (glass-shattering ability required)	☐
F4	2	Solve roman numeral puzzle (explosion and enemy disguise abilities required)	☐
F5	2	Use swords to cut cage chains and collect	☐
F6	3	In alcove beyond tiny door (thuggee chant ability required)	☐
F7	3	Find 5 skulls to get (tiny size and excavate abilities required)	☐
F8	3	Whip-swing across gap near Sir Richard's coffin (Free Play only)	☐
F9	4	Fix far-right crane, then use (repair and explosion abilities required)	☐
10	4	Smash 10 buoys in water to reveal	☐
	1	Navigate area beyond water gate (tiny size ability required)	☐

True Adventurer stud requirement: 50,000 studs

Helpful Free Play Skills:

Enemy disguise ability   Repair ability

Excavate ability   Thuggee chant ability

Explosion ability   Tiny size ability

Glass-shattering ability

STORY MODE CHARACTERS

Indiana Jones (Professor)   **Brody**   **Elsa**

Area 1: Venice Pier

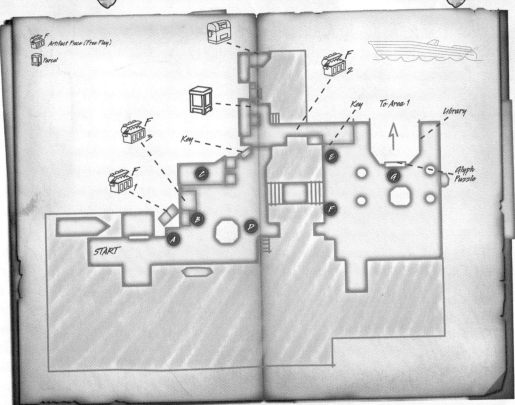

Ah, Venice

The sun is shining in Venice, but you've no time to dally. Switch to Elsa and use her great jumping ability to grab the high, overhead rope here. Climb the rope to reach the balcony above.

Leave Elsa standing on the balcony and switch to either Indy or Brody. Pull the nearby lever to extend the balcony's awing. Now Elsa can bounce across to reach another high balcony.

TIP

Remember to press the jump button when bouncing on awnings to soar even higher.

Once again, leave Elsa standing on this high balcony and switch to Indy or Brody. Pull a second nearby lever to extend some more awnings, then bounce Elsa across.

Nab the key from the farthest balcony, then drop to the street. Run toward the

foreground to find a key mechanism standing here, near the drawbridge. Use the key to activate the mechanism and raise a nearby whip point. Switch to Indy and swing across.

TIP

Jump into the fountains to float upward and claim valuable studs.

Free Play Goodies

Artifact Piece 1

Use a female character's great jumping ability to reach the balcony above the shop near the pier. Then toggle your Free Play character to one who has the glass-shattering ability. Break the balcony's window and nab the artifact piece from inside the building.

Artifact Piece 2

Smash the display case in the ally to the left of the library, then stack the jiggling bits that spill out to form a tiny door on the wall. Toggle to a Free Play character that has the tiny size ability, then crawl through the door to reach the patio above.

Run across the patio and claim an artifact piece that's behind the window to the left.

Parcel

After building the tiny door in the ally to the left of the library, use a tiny size character to reach the patio above and then pull the patio's lever. This raises the gate in the waterway below; swim through to reach a special section of the pier.

Use Indy's whip at the whip point to yank down the parcel, then punch through the nearby boards to discover a lever. Pull the lever to start the nearby lift.

Carry the parcel onto the lift and ride up. Set the parcel down on the balcony and then smash the nearby boards to access two small rooms. Punch open the cupboards in one room to find a key, then use they key on the other room's mechanism to extend a small platform outside.

Pick up the parcel once more and carefully hop across the platform you extended. Hop across the ledges that follow, using Indy's whip to bring the parcel across the wide gap. Deposit the parcel in the nearby postbox, sending it back to Barnett College.

Artifact Piece 3

Use a character with the glass-shattering ability to smash the glass at the pier's far right side and gain access to the moped that's on display.

Pilot the moped, then cruise about and run over all the construction cones that have appeared. Be sure to cross the bridge and hit the cones at the pier's left side as well! You're awarded an artifact piece when all the cones have been destroyed.

Connecting the Bridge

Defeat the fez-wearing men who attack Indy, then destroy the bars here to gain access to a key in the nook beyond.

Use the key at the mechanism here to connect the drawbridge. Now Brody and Elsa can join Indy!

Entering the Library

Stand in front of the library's door and use either Elsa or Brody to solve the glyph puzzle on the wall above. The library door then opens; step inside to reach the next area.

Area 2: Library

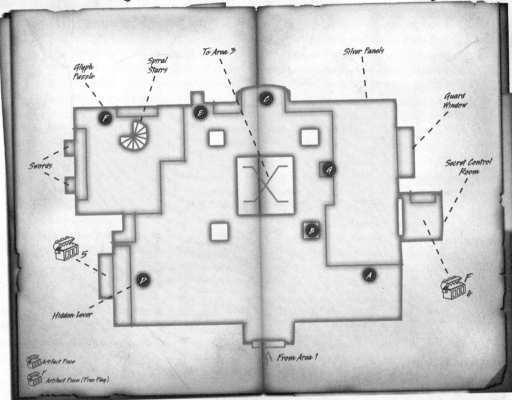

Quiet, Please

All's quiet in the library. Stack the jiggling LEGO bits near the ladder to give the ladder handles, then shove the ladder to the right as far as it will go. Climb up to reach a box of LEGO bits atop a high shelf.

Place the box of bits onto one of the four green pads near the middle of the library. Stack the jiggling bits afterward to add some floor tiles to the library's center. Three more boxes of bits to find!

Hunting for Bits

The second box of LEGO bits sits here, near the stained glass window. Place it on one of the green pads as you did before, then stack the bits to add more central floor tiles.

Punch the colored books on the shelves here to reveal a lever. Pull the lever to spin a nearby bookcase and discover a box of LEGO bits. You know what to do with these!

Exploring Upstairs

To reach the upper balcony, use Indy's whip at the whip point here to tug on a ceiling switch. This causes a spinner to pop up from the floor nearby; push the green side of the spinner's handle to extended the nearby circular staircase, then dash upstairs.

Solve the glyph puzzle near the safe on the second-floor balcony to open the safe and obtain the final box of LEGO bits. Place this on the last remaining green pad, then stack the bits to add the last few tiles to the middle of the library's floor.

Free Play Goodie

Artifact Piece 4

Stack the jiggling bits near the upper balcony's ladder to give the ladder a handle, then push the ladder to the right. Climb up and toggle your Free Play character to one with the enemy disguise ability, then knock on the nearby guard window and let the guard ID you.

The guard opens a secret door to the right, exposing and enemy-filled control room. Defeat the enemies and destroy their equipment to reveal some jiggling LEGO bits. Stack the bits to assemble an odd contraption against the left wall.

Use a character with the explosion ability to destroy the silver panels on the wall near the balcony's ladder. This reveals three Roman numerals. Input these numerals on the control room contraption by jumping onto the levers. An artifact piece appears when the correct code is entered.

X Marks the Spot

With the central floor tiles in place, an overhead handrail and whip point appear. Return upstairs and use the handrail above the stained glass window to cross over to the right side of the balcony.

When you're ready to move on, position Indy at the balcony's whip point and then use his whip to yank on the hanging chandelier. The chandelier comes crashing down, busting through the central floor tiles and revealing a secret passage! Drop into the hole to proceed.

Artifact Piece 5

Smash the large planters near the suit of armor on the ground floor to reveal three piles of jiggling LEGO bits. Stack the bits to complete the checkered floor so you may push the suit of armor onto the pressure plate to the right. This reveals some swords on the balcony above; use the spiral staircase to get up there.

Take one of the swords and use it to cut one of the support bars of the cage that's protecting an artifact piece in a nook above some bookshelves. Use the other sword to cut the other bar to get rid of the cage so you can collect your prize.

Area 3: Sir Richard's Tomb

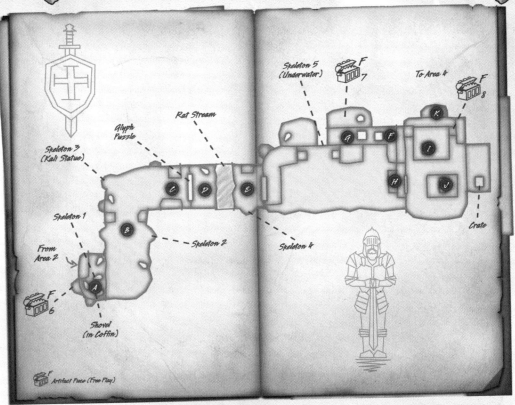

Brilliant Discovery

Indy has managed to locate the long-lost tomb of Sir Richard—a truly amazing find. Now to find Sir Richard himself. Punch the coffins down here to find a shovel that pops out of one, but beware: sharp spikes jut up from most of the other coffins!

Throw torches at high spiderwebs to destroy them and claim some bonus studs.

Use your newfound shovel to dig up a box of LEGO bits from the ground here. Place the box on the green pad ahead, then stack the jiggling bits to form a fan.

Hidden Glyphs

Push against the handle of the large stone object in the wall near the fan, then pull to drag the object out. Jump up and stand atop the object to weigh down its pressure plate and activate the fan.

The fan blows away dust on the nearby wall, revealing a glyph puzzle. Solve the puzzle to open the way forward.

Oh, Rats

Elsa is terrified by the stream of scurrying rats here, but not Indy. Double-jump past the rats as Indy, then grab a torch from one of the sconces on the other side.

Use the torch to light the two braziers on the walls above the rats. This scares off the pests, clearing the way for Elsa to cross.

Have Elsa jump up and grab the high, overhead rope beyond the rats. This allows Indy to pull the lever ahead and open a new path.

Free Play Goodies

Artifact Piece 6

This artifact piece is visible through the bars near the start of the tomb, but it takes some doing to collect. You must find five skeletons in the tomb to remove the bars and get at the artifact piece.

The first skeleton is in a coffin near the artifact piece itself. Hit the coffin to open it and reveal the skeleton.

The second skeleton is in an larger coffin a short distance up the path. Push against the coffin's handle to grab it, then pull back to drag it out. The skeleton pops out.

The third skeleton is linked to the passage's Kali statue. Activate the statue with a character who has the thuggee chant ability. A skeleton then falls from the ceiling.

The fourth skeleton is in an alcove just past the stream of rats. Punch the wooden boards on the right until they smash apart to reveal the skeleton.

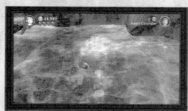

The fifth skeleton is trapped underwater just beyond the stream of rats. Jump into the water and dive down to hit the three underwater valves. Hit them all quickly to make the skeleton float to the surface. With all five skeletons accounted for, return to the area's entrance and collect your prize.

Artifact Piece 7

Have Elsa jump up and grab the overhead rope on the high ledge near the water. This reveals a tiny door that was hidden in the nearby wall. Quickly toggle to a character who's small enough to fit through the little door and crawl through.

After popping out of a matching door in a high alcove, toggle to a character with the excavate ability (assuming you aren't carrying a shovel from earlier). Then dig through the alcove's sparkling ground to drop into a lower alcove, where an artifact piece awaits collection.

Artifact Piece 8

During Free Play mode, solve the crate puzzle near Sir Richard's crypt, then slide the large coffin that pops up from the floor all the way to the left. Now any super jump character can leap from the coffin to reach the left ledge.

Free Play Goodies (continued)

Once atop the ledge, toggle your Free Play character to Indy, then whip-swing across the room to nab an artifact piece.

Pulling out the switch causes a nearby platform to rise, granting you access to a pair of levers. Guide both characters to the platform and pull one of the levers. Your partner automatically pulls the other lever, revealing yet another passage leading deeper into the tomb.

Next, run to the foreground and shove the large coffin all the way to the right until it sinks into place. Then switch to Elsa and use the coffin to help you reach another crate in the ledge above.

Ledges and Levers

Make your way to this high ledge and collect a torch from the nearby wall. Toss the torch at the spiderweb in the corner to reveal a switch.

Have Elsa jump up and grab hold of the overhead rope here to raise two platforms to the right. Quickly switch to Indy and jump up the platforms, then use Indy's whip to tug on the switch you revealed.

Sir Richard's Crypt

At last, you've arrived at Sir Richard's final resting place. Use Indy's whip at the whip point here to yank down an overhead crate, then shove the crate onto one of the two square pressure plates nearby.

TIP

The crate slides a bit even after you stop shoving it. Use short, light shoves to move it more precisely.

Slide the second crate off the ledge and then carefully position it on the other square pressure plate. Once both crates are in place, jump onto one of them. Your partner automatically jumps onto the other, causing a coffin to rise up from the floor.

 *(K)*

When you're ready to leave the crypt, push the coffin toward the background as far as it will go, then switch to Elsa. Jump from the top of the coffin to reach the background alcove, where you discover Sir Richard's remains. You're then taken to the next area.

Area 4: Shipyard

Catching Kazim

Shortly after escaping Sir Richard's tomb, Indy and Elsa are attacked by Kazim at the shipyard. Return fire with your fists until Kazim flees into a motorboat. Dispatch his thugs, then climb aboard one of the other nearby motorboats and hurry after him.

Chase Kazim's boat about the area, ramming his craft to damage it. Slam into Kazim's boat four times to send him crashing onto the central island.

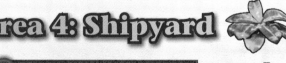

CAUTION

Steer clear of the large ship's propeller at the far-right side of the area. Touching it will destroy your boat!

Map on next page!

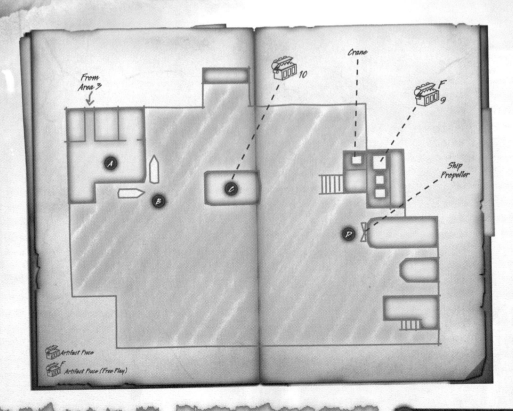

From Area 3

Crane

10

F 9

Ship Propeller

A

B

C

D

Artifact Piece

F Artifact Piece (Free Play)

Free Play Goodie
Artifact Piece 9

Before defeating Kazim, visit the crane at the shipyard's far-right side. Toggle your Free Play character to one with the repair ability, then fix the crane to get it working again. Use the crane to grab and transport your other character onto the nearby high ledge.

Once atop the ledge, jump onto the lower of the two hanging crates. From there, jump onto the handrail of the higher hanging crate. The balance shifts and the lower crate rises; quickly jump across the crates to reach the top of the nearby tower.

Free Play Goodie (continued)

Once atop the tower, toggle to a character with the explosion ability and destroy the silver manhole cover. Then drop through the hole to collect the artifact piece below. To escape, blow up the manhole cover down below, then slide out the drainage pipe.

Showdown: Kazim

Once Kazim is out of his boat, speed to the central island and confront him with your fists. Attack Kazim until he flees into another boat, then return to your own boat and continue the chase.

Ram Kazim's boat as you did before to damage it. This time, Kazim pulls his boat next to the spinning propeller of a giant ship. Jump onto Kazim's boat and punch him a few more times to finish the fight. Level complete!

Artifact Piece 10

While exploring the shipyard by motorboat, smash into the ten buoys floating in the water to reveal an hidden artifact piece atop the central island.

CASTLE RESCUE

Family Reunion

Indiana has learned that his father has been captured by the enemy and is being held prisoner at a remote castle. Without delay, Indiana and Elsa depart for the castle to stage a daring rescue. After acting their way past the butler (and then knocking him out when that plan didn't quite work), Indy and Elsa begin their search for Henry Jones.

STAGE COLLECTIBLES

Item	Area	Notes	Got It?
1	1	Destroy 4 red shield armor suits (explosion ability required)	☐
2	1	On high ledge in secret control room (thuggee chant and tiny size abilities required)	☐
3	1	Destroy silver object near crane (explosion ability required)	☐
4	1	Hovering above shelf near movable table	☐
5	2	Crawl through tiny door to reach (tiny size ability needed)	☐
6	2	Solve glyph puzzle with Henry Jones	☐
7	3	On far ledge left of bazookas	☐
8	3	On scaffolding (blast chain to use ladder)	☐
9	3	In gargoyle statue (push off ledge to break and reveal)	☐
10	3	Blast silver cabinet; complete and solve glyph puzzle	☐
	1	In secret control room (thuggee chant and explosion abilities required)	☐

True Adventurer stud requirement:
35,000 studs

Helpful Free Play Skills:
Explosion ability
Thuggee chant ability
Tiny size ability

STORY MODE CHARACTERS

Indiana Jones   **Elsa**   **Henry Jones**

Area 1: Entry Hall and Outside Wall

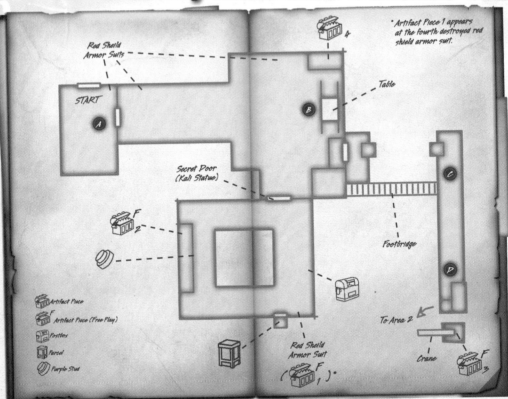

* Artifact Piece 1 appears at the fourth destroyed red shield armor suit.

Red Sheild Armor Suits

START

A

B

Table

Secret Door (Kali Statue)

C

Footbridge

D

F 2

To Area 2

Red Sheild Armor Suit (F 1) *

Crane

F 3

Artifact Piece
F Artifact Piece (Free Play)
Postbox
Parcel
Purple Stud

Storming the Castle

A

All's quiet inside the castle at first. Take a sword from one of the suits of armor along the wall, then throw it at the overhead wire to open the way forward. Defeat the armed guards in the area beyond.

B

Slide the table here all the way to the right, then have Indy use it to reach the whip point above the nearby shelf. Use Indy's whip to open the window, then use the nearby handrail to jump up and out.

Free Play Goodies

Artifact Piece 1

Bring a character with the explosion ability to this level during Free Play mode, then destroy the four suits of armor in the entry hall that have red shields. You'll receive an artifact piece for your trouble!

One of the red shield armor suits is in the secret area linked to the entry

hall's Kali statue. Use a character with the thuggee chant ability to activate the statue and gain entry to the control room beyond. Then blast that last red shield armor suit to win your artifact piece!

Parcel

Pray at the Kali statue to gain entry to the secret control room, then destroy the other suit of armor in the room to reveal some jiggling LEGO bits. Stack the bits to form a key mechanism, then turn the key to lower a rope.

Free Play Goodies (continued)

Hang from the rope to reveal a secret nook where the parcel is hidden. Collect it and drop it into the nearby postbox to send it back to Barnett College.

✋ 🚌 Artifact Piece 2 🚌 🗔

Bash apart two file cabinets in the corner of the secret control room to reveal some LEGO bits. Stack the bits to form tiny door, then toggle your Free Play character to someone who's small enough to crawl through and reach the ledge above. Collect an artifact piece from the far end of the ledge.

Free Play Goodies (continued)

🚌 🚌 Artifact Piece 3 🚌 🚌

Toggle your Free Play character to one who has the explosion ability, then blow up the silver object near the crane. Out pops an artifact piece! Leap over to nab this worthy prize.

This Is Kid's Play

After jumping through the window, whip swing across the gap and defeat the guards. Then stack the nearby jiggling boards to form a bridge so that Elsa can cross as well.

Switch to Elsa and leap onto the high ledge here. Punch the gargoyle statue to destroy it, then stack the jiggling bits that spill out to form a spinner. Push on the green side of the spinner's handle to move the crane across the way.

Once the crane is in position and you're ready to get going, switch to Indy and use his whip at the now-active whip point to advance.

🚌 Artifact Piece 4 🚌

This one's an easy grab: It's just floating above one of the shelves in the entry hall, close to the sliding table. Have Elsa leap up and collect it.

Area 2: Study

Double Crossed

Indy has been reunited with his father, but the two find they have been double-crossed by Elsa. Now they must escape the castle! Smash the chairs and shelves near the glyph puzzle here, then stack the jiggling remains to build a ladder. Climb up and dash across the bookshelves to avoid the flames.

CAUTION

It goes without saying that fire is bad. Don't get too close!

Statues and Shields

Destroy the lamp here, then stack its jiggling remains to add a shield to another nearby statue. Jump and hang from the nearby rope afterward to pull away a curtain, then smash the statue behind the curtain to obtain another shield for the other nearby statue.

Map on next page!

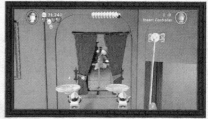

Place the second shield on the other statue, then push against the handle in the wall between the statues to grab hold of it. Pull the handle next to raise the lower statue, then quickly climb the rope and jump across the statues' shields.

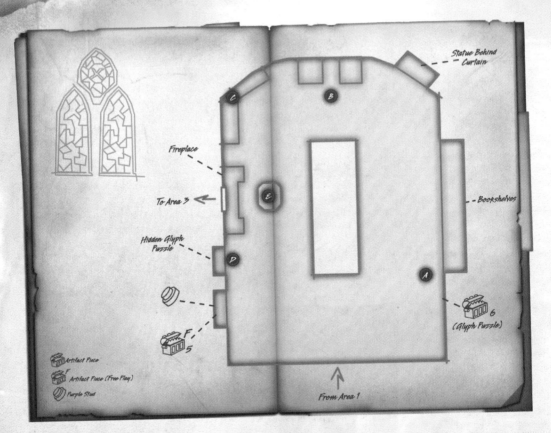

Statue Behind Curtain

Fireplace

To Area 3

Bookshelves

Hidden Glyph Puzzle

6 (Glyph Puzzle)

F 5

Artifact Piece
Artifact Piece (Free Play)
Purple Stud

From Area 1

C

Jump from the second statue and land atop these bookshelves. Run across the bookshelves to slip past the fire below.

Free Play Goodie
Artifact Piece 5

Punch away the books on the shelf past the fireplace to reveal a tiny door. Toggle to a character that's small enough to fit through the door so you may claim the artifact piece that sits atop the shelf, along with a valuable purple stud.

Fireplace Escape

D

Push against the shelf with handles next to the fireplace to slide it inward, revealing a hidden glyph puzzle. Switch to Henry Jones and solve the puzzle to turn the table in front of the fireplace into a spinner.

E

Shove the green side of the spinner table to rotate the fireplace, opening a secret passage through the wall. Sprint through to reach the next area.

Artifact Piece 6

Henry Jones's usefulness is apparent right from the get-go. Use his natural academic ability to solve the glyph puzzle near the start of this area. The puzzle then slides away, revealing a hidden artifact piece!

Area 3: Castle Rooftop

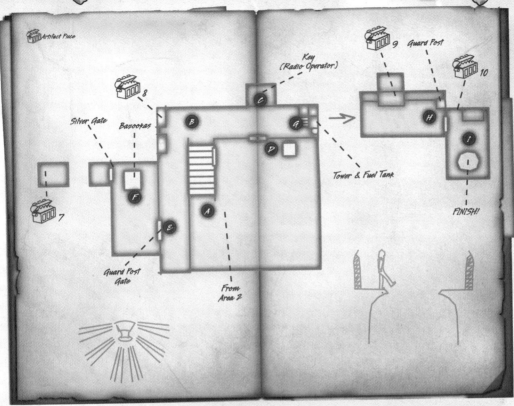

- Artifact Piece
- 8
- Silver Gate
- Bazookas
- 7
- F
- Guard Post Gate
- E
- B
- A
- From Area 2
- C
- Key (Radio Operator)
- D
- G
- Tower & Fuel Tank
- 9 Guard Post
- 10
- H
- I
- FINISH!

Pump Up the Volume

The fireplace passage leads Indy and his dad to a secret enemy control room. Dispatch the guards and then smash everything you see. Find two circular objects and place them on the square object in the corner. Stack the nearby jiggling bits afterward to complete the object: a giant stereo!

After assembling the stereo, turn the nearby key to crank up the volume. The stereo explodes, along with the nearby windows! Dash through the windows to reach the roof.

Showdown: Enemy Radio Operator

Lay into the many soldiers that attack you on the roof. The one near the stairs in the funny headgear is a high-ranking enemy radio operator. Hit him a few times to make him flee upstairs.

Chase the radio operator upstairs and hit him a few more times to make him flee once more. Dispatch his guards and give chase.

Jump onto this platform and deal the radio operator his final blows. Collect the key he leaves behind, then hurry downstairs.

Sound the Alarm!

Use the key on the mechanism near the wall to sound an alarm. More soldiers burst out of the nearby door, backed by an officer. Defeat these enemies and steal the officer's hat.

LEGO INDIANA JONES THE ORIGINAL ADVENTURES

NOTE

Don't worry if you miss the officer's hat. Soldiers will keep coming from the door.

While wearing an enemy officer's hat, return upstairs and knock on the window of the guard post to the left. The guard identifies you and opens the gate, granting you access to a new section of the area.

Pull the lever beyond the guard post to open a nearby trapdoor. A box full of bazookas pops up. Grab one and then backtrack past the guard post.

Blast the fuel tanks near the tower here with your newfound bazooka to topple the tower. Cross the tower like a bridge afterward to reach another rooftop.

Roof Two

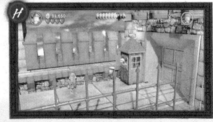

Pound the guards on the second rooftop, then put your enemy officer disguise to use once more at the guard post to the right. Fool the guard to gain entry to the room beyond.

TIP

Lost your officer's hat? Return to the lower portion of the first rooftop and beat up another officer.

It's time to make your escape! Push the little chair along the tile floor as far as it will go to discover a secret staircase, then hurry downstairs. Level complete!

Artifact Piece 7

After acquiring a bazooka, blast the silver gate to the left of the lever and jump across the ledges that follow. The far ledge holds an artifact piece!

Artifact Piece 8

Use a bazooka to blow away the silver chains attached to the ladder near the guard post. Next, climb the ladder to claim the artifact piece that sits atop the scaffolding.

Artifact Piece 9

Shove the gargoyle statue off the second rooftop's high ledge. The statue smashes apart when it lands, revealing an artifact piece!

Artifact Piece 10

Bring a bazooka into the final room past the second guard post and blast the silver cabinet to bits. Collect the glyph tile that's left behind and use it to complete the nearby glyph puzzle. Solve the puzzle with Henry Jones to win a fabulous artifact piece prize.

MOTORCYCLE ESCAPE

Jumping the Border

Despite being doubled-crossed by Elsa, Indiana has helped his father escape the castle where he was being held prisoner. Now the two must make a frantic dash through the countryside, fleeing to safety across the Austrian-German border. This sort of adventure is a new experience for Henry Jones Sr., but it happens to Indy all the time!

STAGE COLLECTIBLES

Item	Area	Notes	Got It?
1	1	In right alley (use boat to reach; explosion and super jump abilities required)	☐
2	1	In back room (explosion and glass-shattering abilities required to get tiles; push object to reveal)	☐
3	2	In alcove near mines (blow up silver boards; explosion ability required)	☐
4	2	Destroy three special roadside plants to grow flowers and reveal	☐
5	2	In barn with open door near second guard post	☐
6	3	Use tractor to find carrots in gardens (repair ability required)	☐
7	3	Behind large stone barn near start	☐
8	3	In the well (turn the key to raise the bucket and reveal)	☐
9	4	Hidden in foreground gun turret (collect after destroying turret)	☐
10	4	Destroy manhole covers with bazooka; plant flower seeds to reveal	☐
	3	Atop windmill (find key, start windmill, super jump from crate to collect)	☐

True Adventurer stud requirement:
75,000 studs

Helpful Free Play Skills:

Explosion ability

Glass-shattering ability

Super jump ability

STORY MODE CHARACTERS

Indiana Jones   Henry Jones

Area 1: Castle Garage

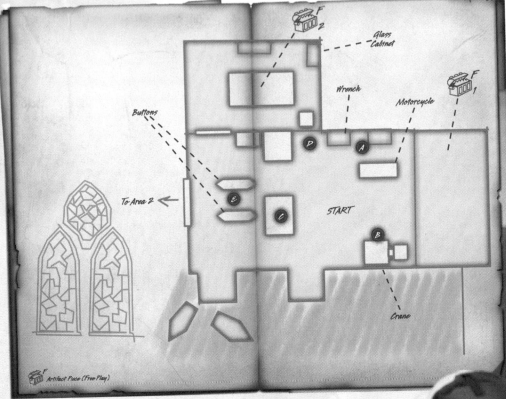

Glass Cabinet

Wrench

Motorcycle

Buttons

To Area 2

START

Artifact Piece (Free Play)

Not Going in the Boat

Time to find a ride and get outta here! Smash a crate against the far wall to discover some jiggling LEGO bits, then stack the bits to form a lever. Pull the lever to lower the nearby motorcycle so you may ride it.

Don't hop on the bike just yet. Instead, smash some more nearby crates to reveal additional jiggling bits. Stack these bits to add a spinner handle to the nearby crane, then push against the handle's green side to rotate the crane and drop its crate on the ground close by.

Pick up the crate and set it down on one of the two green pads here. One more crate to find!

Free Play Goodies

Artifact Piece 1

Use a character with the explosion ability to blow up the silver chains holding the boats at dock. Pilot a boat and go right to find a small secret alley. Jump out of the boat and into the alley, then use a super jump character to collect the artifact piece hovering high overhead.

Artifact Piece 2

Use an explosion ability character to blow up the silver chains holding closed the gate that leads to the garage's back room. Then use a character with the glass-shattering ability to smash open the glass cabinet so you may collect the floor tiles from within.

Free Play Goodies (continued)

Place the floor tiles on the ground where indicated to splay them out. Then shove the movable object along the tiles to open the trapdoor in the middle of the floor. Hey, there's an artifact piece hiding down there!

Building a Bike

Yank the lever near the conveyer belt to start it running. A crate comes rolling out. Place this second crate on the other green pad, then stack the jiggling LEGO bits to build a motorcycle—with a sidecar!

Punch open the drawers of the nearby cabinet to discover a wrench. Collect the wrench and use it to finish repairs on the sidecar bike.

With both motorcycles up and running, jump into one and drive it onto one of the two big buttons on the floor. Indy's dad does the same, causing the garage door to swing open. Speed off before the guards catch up with you!

Area 2: Country Road

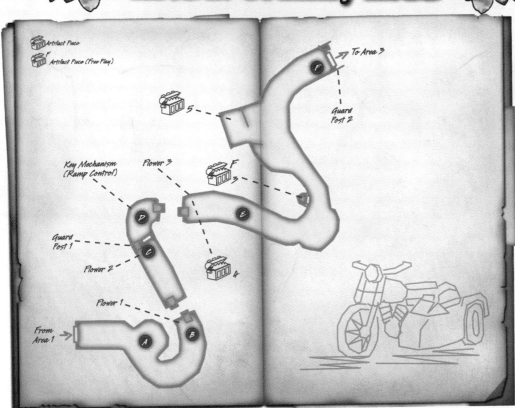

Artifact Piece
Artifact Piece (Free Play)

5
To Area 3
Guard Post 2
Key Mechanism (Ramp Control)
Flower 3
F
3
E
Guard Post 1
D
C
Flower 2
4
Flower 1
From Area 1
A
B

Soldiers Strike

It doesn't take long for enemy soldiers to ambush Indy and his dad along the road. They emerge from this small lot. Either speed away or stand and fight.

Steer clear of the deep mud pits along the road. They'll slow your bikes down, and you'll drown in them if you're on foot!

Pop a wheelie to gain some speed as you approach this gap in the road. Launch off the ramp at top speed to clear the gap with ease.

Guard Post

You encounter a guard post a short distance beyond the jump. Get off your bike and beat up the soldiers that come running down the hill. One is an enemy officer dressed in black. Steal his hat after you defeat him to gain a disguise, then fool the guard at the gate so you may hop on your bike and keep going.

NOTE

Don't worry if you don't get the officer's hat—another officer will eventually emerge from the hill.

Turn the key mechanism just past the guard post to elevate the ramp near the gap ahead. Return to your bike and pop a wheelie to help you soar off the ramp and clear the distance.

Slow down a bit after making the jump and beware the proximity mines down the next stretch. Quickly return to your bike if one blows up and knocks you off, and press onward.

Free Play Goodie
Artifact Piece 3

Use a character with the explosion ability to blow up some silver bars near the proximity mines. Enter the small alcove beyond to collect an artifact piece.

Final Gate

If you kept your officer's disguise, use it once again to get past the final guard gate. If you died and lost the officer's hat, wait for another officer to approach on a bike, then defeat him and claim another disguise.

Artifact Piece 4

Smash through the roadside plants as you motor through this area to uncover three secret flowers. Find all three to win an artifact piece! Check the map for their locations.

Artifact Piece 5

Find an artifact piece inside an open barn not far from the second guard post.

Area 3: Farm

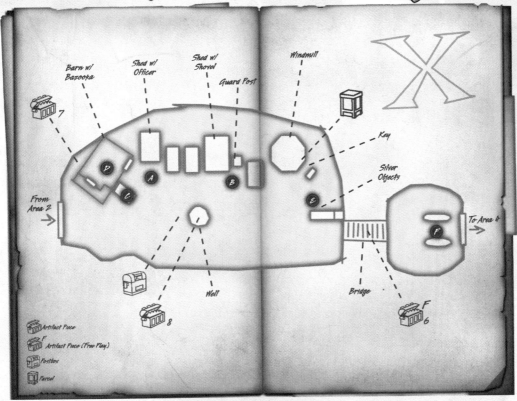

- Barn w/ Bazooka
- Shed w/ Officer
- Shed w/ Shovel
- Guard Post
- Windmill
- Key
- Silver Objects
- From Area 2
- To Area 4
- Bridge
- Well

Artifact Piece
Artifact Piece (Free Play)
Postbox
Parcel

Growing Dangerous

The soldiers continue their pursuit of Indy and his dad into this large farm area. Defeat the first group, then pull the levers on the shed here to open it. More soldiers come pouring out of the shed, along with an officer. Defeat these enemies and steal the officer's hat to claim a disguise.

NOTE

If you ever lose the officer's hat, another officer will emerge from the shed.

Hurry to the guard post here and show the soldier at the window that you're "one of them." He opens the nearby shed, granting you access to the shovel housed within.

Take the shovel and use it to dig up a springboard from the flower bed here, in front of the large stone barn. Bounce off the springboard to reach the barn's high balcony, then enter the barn through the second-floor window.

Barnstorming

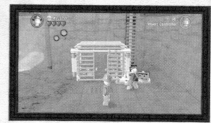

Once inside the barn, whip-swing to the far end of the loft and smash some crates to find a box of LEGO bits. Pick up the box and drop to the ground.

Place the bits on the green pad in front of the barn's metal cage and then stack them to build a handle. Push against the handle to slide open the cage door, then collect the bazooka from within. Exit the barn with this powerful weapon.

Free Play Goodies
🔧 Artifact Piece 6 🔧

Use a character with the repair ability to fix the tractor in the large stone barn, then drive out through the garage door. Till three veggie gardens near the sheds to cause three big carrots to grow and reveal an artifact piece near the bridge!

📦 Parcel 📦

Smash some objects near the farm area's windmill to discover a key. Insert this key into the nearby mechanism, then turn it to start the windmill.

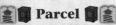

Keep turning the key until a crate pops out of the windmill's lower door.

Free Play Goodies (Continued)

Pick up the crate and place it on the nearby green pad, then toggle your character to one with the super jump ability. Leap from the crate to reach the parcel on the windmill's balcony, then carry the parcel over to the postbox (located near the well) and mail it back to Barnett College.

Bazooka Jones

Don't get caught up in a bazooka fight with the outside soldiers. You only have a few shots, so save your ammo and hurry over to the suspension bridge to the right. Use your bazooka to blow up the silver objects near the bridge to reduce them to jiggling LEGO bits, then stack those bits to build a handle. Push against the handle to grab it, then pull it backward to raise the bridge.

Return to your motorcycle and race across the bridge. Park on one of the two large buttons in front of the gate and wait for your partner to do the same. The gate then opens. Speed into the next area.

🔧 Artifact Piece 7 🔧

Here's another easy one: Simply search behind the large stone barn to discover an artifact piece hidden there.

🔧 Artifact Piece 8 🔧

Turn the key on the central well to raise its bucket. Well, what do you know? There was an artifact piece down there!

Area 4: Border Station

Two Routes

The road forks past the bridge and more soldiers assault Indy and his dad. There's nothing much to see here. Take either path as you race for the far gate, which leads to the compound's interior.

Homeland Security

Soldiers armed with bazookas man three separate gun turrets in this wide-open area. You can't harm the gun turrets or their operators yet. You must first dispatch three groups of motorcycle soldiers that emerge from the compound's sheds.

After the third wave of soldiers emerges from this large shed, enter the shed to collect a bazooka from within. Use the bazooka to destroy the three gun turrets, returning to the shed for a new bazooka each time you run out of ammo.

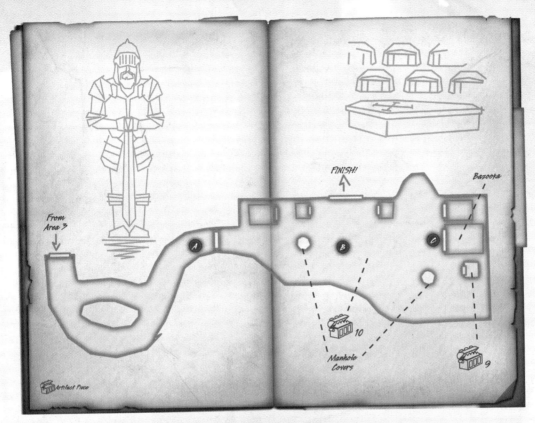

CAUTION

As you destroy the gun turrets, waves of bazooka-armed soldiers pour out from the sheds. It's easy to lose lots of studs here if you aren't quick to take them out!

It takes four shots from a bazooka to destroy each turret. Waste all three of them to open the gate, then hurry through to freedom. Level complete!

Artifact Piece 9

After destroying the foreground gun turret, search the turret's base to discover an artifact piece tucked away inside.

Artifact Piece 10

Use a bazooka to destroy the two manhole covers on the compound's ground. Flowers and seeds come flying out after you do so—plant all of the jiggling seeds to reveal a secret artifact piece!

TROUBLE IN THE SKY

Escape from the Lion's Den

The Jones boys have made good their escape from enemy territory. After a slight detour to retrieve the Grail diary from Elsa, Indiana and his dad prepare to leave Germany once and for all—by blimp! Enemy soldiers are crawling all over the place, though, and the villainous Colonel Vogel yearns to deal with the two Joneses personally. This is gonna be one heck of a ride!

STORY MODE CHARACTERS

Indiana Jones **Henry Jones**

STAGE COLLECTIBLES

Item	Area	Notes	Got It?
1	1	In glass case (super jump and glass-shattering abilities required)	☐
2	2	In house with clock (explosion ability required to find key)	☐
3	2	In shed (use whip to yank down shed handle from water tower)	☐
4	3	On high ledge (explosion and tiny size abilities required)	☐
5	3	On high ledge (solve glyph puzzle to reveal handrails)	☐
6	3	Inside shed (fill silver cart with grain; jump to lever)	☐
7	4	On high ledge (leap along handrails to reach)	☐
8	4	Dig up three sand castles to collect	☐
9	4	Behind boulder at far-right end of beach	☐
10	4	Atop far-right isle (jump up ledges)	☐
	2	Use tractor to uncover three mushrooms; destroy to get	☐

True Adventurer stud requirement:
80,000 studs

Helpful Free Play Skills:

Explosion ability

Glass-shattering ability

Super jump ability

Tiny size ability

Area 1: Blimp Lounge

Ticket, Please

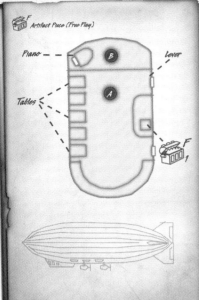

Enemy officers are swarming the blimp's lounge and it's only a matter of time before they make a move. Act first by either punching a patrolling officer or pulling the nearby lever on the wall. Either course of action causes the background curtain to withdraw, revealing a stage.

Colonel Vogel leaps onto the stage and begins tossing chairs at you from afar. Return fire by snatching a glass bottle from a nearby table and tossing it back at the evil man.

TIP

Defeat enemy officers for hearts as needed.

Free Play Goodie

Artifact Piece 1

Return to this level in Free Play mode and use a character with the super jump ability to hop the fence and reach an artifact piece that sits in a glass container to the right. Toggle to a character with the glass-shattering ability, then smash the container and claim your prize.

No Ticket

Keep hitting Vogel with bottles until he loses patience, leaps off the stage, and attacks you directly. Finish with fisticuffs to advance the plot.

Area 2: Crash Site

Nice Landing

Indy and his dad steal the blimp's plane but end up getting "shot down." Punch the downed plane to loosen its propeller motor, then place the motor on the nearby green pad to reduce it to bits.

Stack the bits to create a propeller that blows an updraft. Jump into the updraft to soar up and over the fence to the left.

Claiming the Cog

Use Indy's whip at both whip points here to yank open the gate and tug down a ladder. Climb the ladder to reach the loft above, then leap over to the roof of the nearby house.

Map on next page!

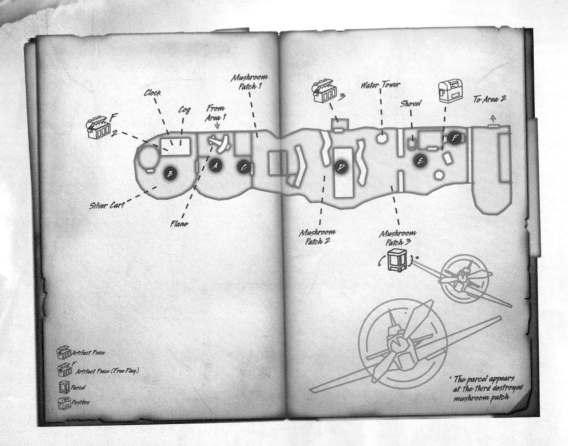

Clock
Cog
From Area 1
Mushroom Patch 1
Water Tower
Shovel
To Area 2
F
2
B
A
C
Silver Cart
Plane
D
E
F
Mushroom Patch 2
Mushroom Patch 3

* The parcel appears at the third destroyed mushroom patch

Artifact Piece

Artifact Piece (Free Play)

Parcel

Postbox

Punch the clock on the house's roof to reduce it to jiggling bits. Stack the bits to reform the clock if you wish, then collect the cog that has fallen free.

Carry the cog to the lever near the gate to the right. Fit the cog into place and then yank the lever to open the gate.

Free Play Goodies

Artifact Piece 2

After punching the rooftop clock and reassembling it, toggle to a Free Play character with the explosion ability and blast the nearby silver cart. Collect the key that spills out of the cart, then insert it into the mechanism on the house's porch. Turn the key to change the clock's time to 12:45 (which is scrawled on the house) to open the house's front door and collect the artifact piece inside.

Parcel

Hop into the driver's seat of the tractor that only appears in this area during Free Play. Drive the tractor over three patches of plants that you're unable to smash with your fists. (Check the map to find their locations). A mushroom pops up from each patch you driver over. Attack the mushrooms to destroy them.

This level's parcel appears right next to you after you destroy the third mushroom. Drop the parcel into the nearby postbox to send it back to Barnett College.

Dad, They're Coming Back

Head's up: Bombs begin falling as you dash past the gate, along with groups of enemy paratroopers! Keep away from the bombs after they touch down and beat up each trooper group as you cut through the field.

Punch your way into the tiny shed here to find a shovel stashed within. Take the shove and dig at the nearby patch of glowing soil to unearth a platform, then jump up and grab the nearby rope. This starts the platform moving up and down like and elevator.

Use the lift platform to reach the top of the shed, then jump to grab the rope that's hanging to the right. Leap from the rope and land on the wooden platform, then quickly jump over the high wall to reach an orchard. Sprint along the background path to reach the next area.

CAUTION

The wooden platform collapses just seconds after you land on it. Jump fast or you'll need to stack the platform's bits to reassemble it and try again.

TIP

Punch the apples hanging from the orchard trees for bonus studs!

Artifact Piece 3

Use Indy's whip at the whip point beneath the water tower to yank down a blue object. Place this object on the door of the shed to the left to give the door a handle. The door then opens, granting you access to the shed's artifact piece!

Area 3: Countryside

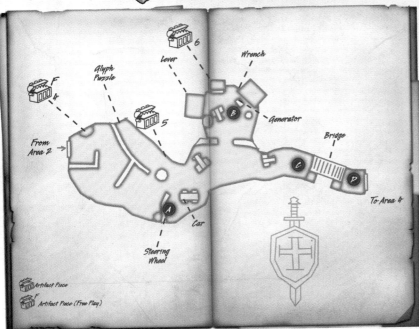

Glyph Puzzle

Lever

6

Wrench

F
4

5

From Area 2

Generator

Bridge

To Area 4

A

Car

Steering Wheel

Artifact Piece

Artifact Piece (Free Play)

Arranging Transportation

Bombs and paratroopers continue to drop in this area, so hurry over to the broken car here. Stack the jiggling bits to piece the car back together, then smash a nearby wagon to discover the car's steering wheel. Place the steering wheel on the car to finish its assembly. Now you just need to find a wrench and repair it!

Destroy three blue tractors in this area to discover three batteries. Place each tractor battery on the device here, near a generator.

After you place all three batteries, a button pops out of the device. Jump onto the button to start the generator, which causes a ladder to extend up the wall of the nearby house. Climb up the ladder and claim the wrench from the house's high balcony, then return to the car and complete its repairs.

Free Play Goodie
Artifact Piece 4

Smash the rubble near this area's entry point to reveal a tiny door. Switch to a small character and crawl through to reach a ledge high above, where you discover an artifact piece.

Bridge Out!

Jump into the car and speed along the street until you reach a broken bridge. Hop out and use Indy's whip to swing across the gap.

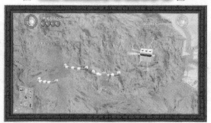

Smash a stack of wooden pallets across the bridge, then stack the jiggling LEGO bits to restore the bridge's missing planks. Return to the car, speed across the bridge and smash through the fence to reach the final area.

Artifact Piece 5

Have Henry Jones solve the glyph puzzle up the hill to extend a series of handrails from

the nearby rock wall. Leap up and grab onto the lowest handrail, then jump across to a far ledge, where an artifact piece awaits.

Artifact Piece 6

Grab hold of the silver wagon near the house and sheds, then pull the wagon to the right as far as you can. Move to the wagon's other side and then push the wagon to the right until it can go no farther. Once the wagon is in place, grain begins falling from the tall silo, filling the wagon completely.

When the wagon is full of grain, pull it back over to the left. Jump on top of the wagon, then leap onto the loft of the nearby barn. Pull the lever in the loft to open the door of the nearby shed, gaining access to a hidden artifact piece!

Area 4: Seagull Beach

Birds in the Sky

The Jones boys lose their car during their frantic dash through the tunnel. Rush down the zigzagging path on foot, pummeling each group of enemy soldiers you encounter along the way.

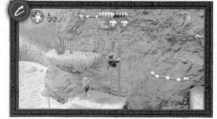

You end up scaring a flock of seagulls at the bottom of the path. The seagulls fly up and get caught in the propeller of the enemy plane that's been dropping paratroopers and bombs at you. Two more flocks to find!

The Second Flock

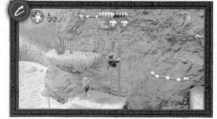

Leap up the rocks here and climb up the ladder on the rock wall. Jump along the handrails that follow, making your way to the right.

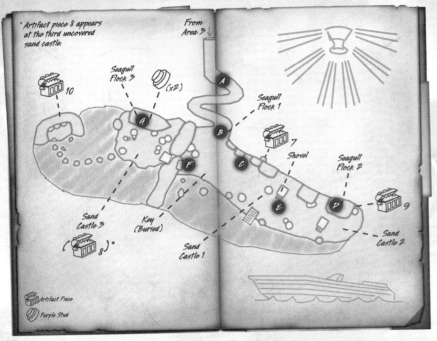

* Artifact piece 8 appears at the third uncovered sand castle.

From Area 3

Seagull Flock 3
(x2)
10
Seagull Flock 1
A
B
7
C
Shovel
Seagull Flock 2
F
E
D
9
Sand Castle 3
Key (Buried)
8
Sand Castle 1
Sand Castle 2

Artifact Piece
Purple Stud

Use a hanging vine to reach this far ledge, where the second flock of seagulls awaits. The seagulls flee when they see you—right into the enemy plane's propellers!

The Third Flock

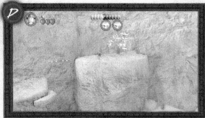

Find a shovel sitting near this shack, then use it to dig up a chest that's buried in the sand to the left. Whack the chest to open it and take the key you discover within.

Insert the key into the mechanism here, then turn it to extend some nearby steps. Scale the steps to reach the left side of the shore.

Use the handrail of the ship that's washed up on shore here to board its deck, then leap up to the roof of the ship's cabin to scare away the third and final flock of seagulls. The enemy plane's propeller becomes totally jammed and the plane goes down in feathers and flames. Level complete!

Artifact Piece 7

Climb the ladder on the rock wall to the right of the first group of seagulls, then leap up the handrails that follow. You eventually arrive at a high ledge that sports an artifact piece!

Artifact Piece 8

Use the shovel you find near one of the shacks to dig up three sand castles buried along the beach. (Check the map for their locations.) Uncover all three castles and you're awarded a fabulous artifact piece prize!

Artifact Piece 9

Nothing tricky about this one: Simply sprint to the far-right end of the beach and search behind a boulder to discover an artifact piece.

Artifact Piece 10

Before scaring off the third flock of seagulls, head into the foreground and follow the trail of rocks that sticks out from the water to discover a secluded isle. Leap up the isle's ledges to reach an artifact piece that's siting way up on top.

DESERT AMBUSH

The Brotherhood Returns

Indiana has tracked Donovan and his evil cohorts all the way to the desert. As Indy and Sallah spy on the convoy from a distant embankment, they're shocked to see that Donovan has enlisted the aid of a fearsome tank! A gleam off Indy's binoculars accidently gives away his location, but just then, bullets start whizzing by—Kazim's brotherhood has reappeared! The fez-wearing men begin an all-out assault on the would-be Grail thieves, and Indiana hurries to join in the fight.

STAGE COLLECTIBLES

Item	Area	Notes	Got It?
1	1	In secret cavern beyond glyph puzzle (academic, explosion, and thuggee chant abilities required)	❑
2	1	Highest ledge in cave (explosion ability required)	❑
3	1	Inside the cave (fix lion head statue)	❑
4	1	Atop high left ledge (jump off a horse to reach)	❑
5	1	Find and ram 3 silver poles in bulldozer	❑
6	2	Build oil drill to reveal	❑
7	2	Build water sprinkler to reveal (trick Vogel)	❑
8	2	Fix mine cart, then shove to access	❑
9	3	Crawl through tiny door to reach (tiny size ability required)	❑
10	3	Find key in silver crate; raise ledge platform and hop across	❑
	2	Leap from crate before shoving off ledge to get (super jump ability required)	❑

True Adventurer stud requirement:
100,000 studs

Helpful Free Play Skills:

 Academic ability

 Explosion ability

Super jump ability

Thuggee chant ability

Tiny size ability

STORY MODE CHARACTERS

Indiana Jones   Sallah (Fez)

Area 1: Canyon A

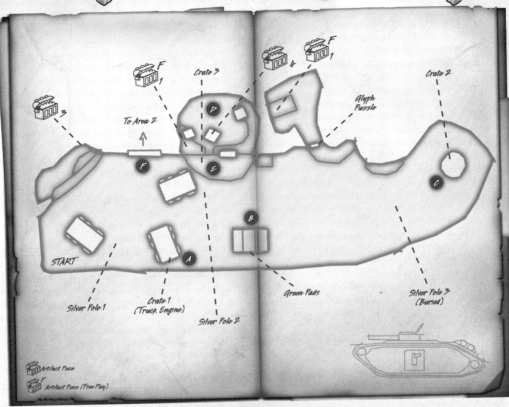

Artifact Piece
Artifact Piece (Free Play)

Pitched Battle

Kazim's brotherhood has done a number on the enemy convoy—the tank is nowhere in sight, but many of their trucks lie in ruin. Dispatch the nearby enemy soldiers, then work at dismantling the truck here with Indy's fist. Smash all of the truck's tires and break the engine block, then stack the jiggling bits that remain to form a large crate.

NOTE

Kazim's men are on your side this time. They help fight the enemy and won't attack you.

Pick up the crate you built out of truck parts and carry it to the trio of green pads to the right. Set the crate down on one of the pads. Two more crates to find!

The Second Crate

The second crate you need sits atop a skinny pillar at the far-right side of the canyon. Mount the nearby horse, then jump from the saddle to have the horse buck you up and onto the pillar. Collect the crate and return to the green pads to place it.

The Third Crate

Enter the canyon's cave and have Sallah dig at the glowing patch of soil therein to discover some jiggling cogs. Stack the cogs to repair the nearby mechanism, which automatically activates the cave's lift. Step onto the lift when it lowers and then ride up to the path above.

Exit the cave through its upper opening to reach a high outdoor ledge. The third crate is located here. Place it on the nearby lift to lower it to the ground, then ride down yourself.

Free Play Goodies

Artifact Piece 1

Punch some steel barrels near the cliff to destroy them and reveal some jiggling LEGO bits. Stack those bits to build a ladder leading up to a ledge, then climb up. Use a character with the academic ability to solve the glyph puzzle, then enter the secret cavern beyond!

Use a character with the explosion ability to clear out the silver wreckage inside the cavern. Then toggle to a character who has the thuggee chant ability and pray at the cavern's Kali statue. The walls begin to rumble, causing some tiles to fall.

Stack the tiles that have fallen near the lion statue to complete the checkered floor. Then slide the lion statue back against the wall to reveal a hidden dig spot! Switch to Sallah and dig there to unearth a long-lost artifact piece. Well done!

Artifact Piece 2

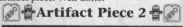

Use a character who has the explosion ability to blow up the silver crates inside the canyon's cave, revealing a key. Take the key, then use the cave's lift to reach the upper ledges.

Free Play Goodies (continued)

Use the key at the mechanism on the farthest ledge to activate the nearby whip point. Then use Indy's whip to swing across the cave, landing on a remote ledge. Destroy the rocks here to reveal an artifact piece. Don't miss the nearby purple stud!

Joy Ride

With all three crates accounted for, stack the massive pile of jiggling bits to form a bulldozer. Pilot the dozer, and when you're ready to move on, smash through the heavy barricade here to advance to the next area.

Artifact Piece 3

Enter the canyon's cave to discover a broken lion statue. Pick up the lion's head and return it to its body to repair the statue and discover a hidden artifact piece!

Artifact Piece 4

Ride the horse across the canyon to the cliffs at its far-left side. Lead the horse right up to the cliffs, then jump from the saddle to make the horse buck you way up to the second ledge.

Once you're atop the second ledge, use the overhead handrail to reach the ledge above, where an artifact piece awaits.

Artifact Piece 5

After assembling the bulldozer, take a moment to find and destroy three silver poles in the canyon. The first is near the start point, the second must be assembled out of jiggling bits, and the third lies buried and must be excavated by Sallah. Check the map to find their locations and ram all three to win an artifact piece!

Area 2: Tank Showdown

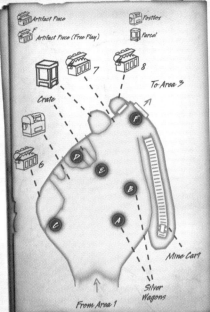

Colonel Vogel periodically tries to run you down by steering his tank all over the place. When he passes near the mines you've built, the mines explode and his tank suffers damage. One more mine to find!

Free Play Goodie

Parcel

Before shoving the crate off the ledge to build the final proximity mine, toggle to a female character, then use her superior jumping ability to leap from the crate and grab hold of the handrail above. Use the handrails to reach this level's parcel, which sits atop the nearby ledge.

Carry the parcel to the ground and switch to Sallah. Dig at the patch of glowing sand beneath the weak, wooden boards to uncover the postbox, then mail the parcel back to Barnett College.

The Final Mine

Stack the jiggling LEGO bits here to build a ladder, then hurry up to the ledge above.

Leap across the ledges (beware of those weak boards!) until you reach this ledge, where a crate sits. Shove the crate off the ledge to smash it on the ground below.

E

Drop to the ground and stack the crate's jiggling remains to form the third and final proximity mine. Colonel Vogel's tank is damaged by the mine the next time he drives about.

F

Having suffered enough, Vogel speeds off in his tank, smashing through a barricade here and fleeing into the next area. Finish looting the area if you like, then hurry after him!

Besting the Steel Beast

Indy and Sallah don't get far on their bulldozer—Colonel Vogel obliterates their dozer with a shot from his tank bazooka. Bait Vogel into firing at the wagon full of silver fuel tanks here, then stack the jiggling remains to create a proximity mine.

B

Trick Colonel Vogel into destroying the other wagon here and stack its remains to form a second proximity mine.

Artifact Piece 6

Build and climb the area's ladder, then stand near the silver tank above and trick Colonel Vogel into firing at you. Stack the jiggling LEGO bits that are left behind to build a large oil drill.

The drill starts up automatically once it's built, and oil begins to spurt out everywhere. Hang around a while until an artifact piece shoots up as well! Jump into the oily fountain to ride upward to claim this special prize.

Artifact Piece 7

Bait Colonel Vogel into firing at the silver fuel tanks against the far background wall. This reveals some jiggling LEGO bits—stack them to build a water sprinkler.

The sprinkler starts up and causes some flowers and grass to grow. Then it explodes into an artifact piece! Collect this treasure, and then destroy the flora for bonus studs.

Artifact Piece 8

Run along the track to the right of the area to discover a broken mine cart at the far end. Use Sallah to dig up some jiggling bits from the nearby glowing soil, then stack the bits to complete the mine cart.

Shove the mine cart after it's fully assembled to send it crashing through the loose rocks down the hill. Now you can collect the artifact piece that was hiding in the nook beyond!

Area 3: Canyon B

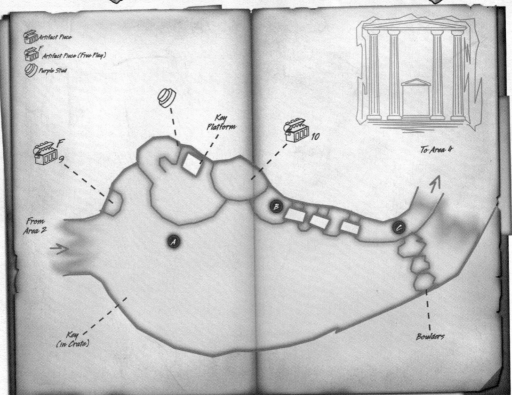

Vogel's Revenge

Vogel's tank has suffered damage from your mines, but that doesn't stop the wicked colonel from attacking you in this next stretch of canyon. Avoid his bazooka blasts and mount one of the nearby horses. Jump from the saddle to have the horse buck you onto one of the high background ledges.

Beware: Colonel Vogel can still harm you up here! Jump to the right, hopping across the smaller ledges. Avoid those weak, wooden boards!

If you fall, use a horse to get back up to the ledges.

Keep moving right until you reach this final ledge. During his pursuit, Vogel smashes through the giant boulders below and speeds off. Continue moving to the right to reach the next area.

Free Play Goodie
Artifact Piece 9

During Free Play mode, send a bite-size character crawling through the tiny door near the entrance to Canyon B to reach a high, overhead ledge. Collect the artifact piece you discover up there.

Artifact Piece 10

Trick Colonel Vogel into firing at the silver crate near the entrance to Canyon B, then collect the key that pops out.

Jump from a horse to reach the high, background ledges, then use the key at the mechanism to raise a metal platform. Run up the path and leap across the raised platform to reach an even higher ledge, where an artifact piece awaits collection.

Area 4: Tank Chase

Showdown: Colonel Vogel

Indy and Sallah make a daring leap from a high ledge and land atop Vogel's tank. It's time to teach this villain a lesson! Remain on the tank and dispatch each truckload of enemy soldiers that pulls up and hops aboard.

After you defeat a few groups of soldiers, Colonel Vogel emerges from the tank and tries to deal with you himself. Hit the wicked colonel as many times as you can before he retreats into the belly of his steel beast once more.

Many more trucks pull up and unload soldiers onto the tank. Keep those fists flying and wipe out each truckload as quickly as you can, then punish Vogel each time he pops up to face you. Rinse and repeat until Vogel is no more. Level complete!

TEMPLE OF THE GRAIL

Enemy at the Gate

This is it—the final showdown between good and evil! Indiana and his entourage have tracked Donovan's caravan all the way through the Canyon of the Crescent Moon, and they now stand ready to ambush Donovan's men at the Temple of the Grail's front entrance. The time for subtly is past—Donovan must not be allowed to possess the Grail!

STAGE COLLECTIBLES

Treasure	Area	Notes	Got It?
1	1	On high ledge (jump from horse to reach)	☐
2	2	In nook near Kali statue (thuggee chant ability required)	☐
3	3	In secret chamber (tiny size ability required)	☐
4	3	In nook beyond cage (cut rope with sword character)	☐
5	3	In nook beyond the first bridge	☐
6	4	On high ledge (tiny size ability required)	☐
7	4	On high ledge (repair ability required to fix generator)	☐
8	5	In lion's mouth (explosion ability required)	☐
9	5	Beneath second ledge's grate (use whip to get)	☐
10	5	On fourth ledge (light torch; solve glyph puzzle)	☐
	1	Buried near start (explosion ability required to find postbox)	☐

True Adventurer stud requirement:
80,000 studs

Helpful Free Play Skills:

Explosion ability

Repair ability

Thuggee chant ability

Tiny size ability

STORY MODE CHARACTERS

Indiana Jones   **Henry Jones**

Sallah (Fez)   **Brody**

Area 1: Temple Entrance

Free Play Goodie

📦 Parcel 📦

Have Sallah dig at the patch of glowing soil near the foreground to uncover this level's parcel. That was easy!

Unfortunately, finding the postbox is a bit tougher. Return to this level in Free Play mode and use a character with the explosion ability to blow up the enemy trucks. Jiggling bits spill out of the right truck. Stack them to build the postbox, then mail the parcel back to Barnett College.

⚜ Artifact Piece 1 ⚜

Hop the stable's fence and mount a horse, then jump from the saddle to reach a high, overhead handrail. Leap from the handrail to reach the nearby ledge, where you discover a purple stud and a key.

Use the key to open the stable gate, then ride a horse toward the foreground. Look up to spy an artifact piece sitting on a high ledge. Position the horse near the ledge, then leap from the saddle to get up there and claim your prize. You also find two purple studs on the ledge—bonus!

So Many Soldiers

Look at all those soldiers! Rush forward and whack the support poles at the backs of the enemy trucks ahead. This closes the trucks' back doors, stemming the tide of enemies.

Switch to Sallah and dig up an odd shrine from the sparkling ground here. Smash the shrine to reveal some jiggling LEGO bits, then stack the bits to build a ladder on the rock wall.

Entering the Temple

Take control of either Henry Jones or Brody, then climb up the ladder. Use the handrail and rope that follow to reach the top of the temple, then solve the glyph puzzle you find up there. The middle of the temple's roof then rises, allowing you to continue across.

Cross the temple's roof and solve the left glyph puzzle to reveal two levers near the temple's front door. Pull the levers to open the door and gain entry to the temple.

Area 2: Hall of the Great Seal

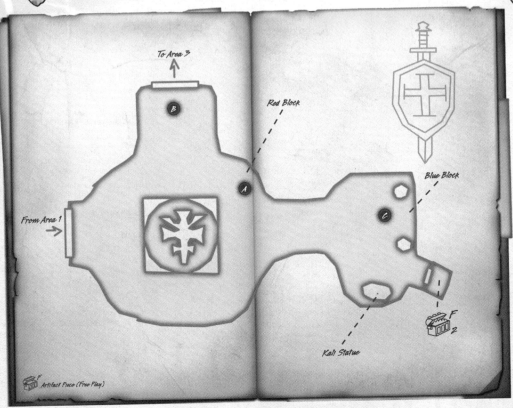

To Area 3

Red Block

Blue Block

From Area 1

A

B

C

Kali Statue

F
2

F Artifact Piece (Free Play)

Sacred Place

All's quiet inside the temple. Donovan is nowhere in sight. Bash the odd shrine here to reveal a sparkling patch of soil, then have Sallah dig there to uncover a red block.

Carry the red block over to the door and place it on the left column where indicated. One more block to find!

Free Play Goodie
Artifact Piece 2

During Free Play mode, chant at the Kali statue with a character who has the thuggee chant ability to reveal a hidden nook containing an artifact piece.

The Blue Block

Snatch a torch from one of the sconces on the walls, then use it to light the brazier near the wall here. The extra light it gives reveals a glyph puzzle on the wall above. Solve the puzzle with Henry Jones or Brody to acquire the blue block, then place the block near the door as you did before to open the way forward.

Area 3: Cavern of Trials

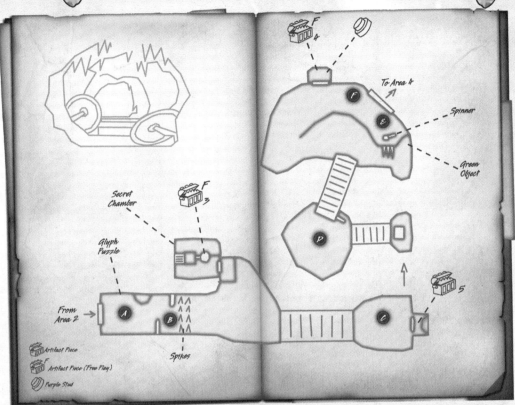

The Penitent Man Shall Pass

Curse that evil Donovan! He's shot Indy's dad, forcing our hero to recover the Grail to save his father. Fortunately, Indy now possesses the Grail diary. Use it to solve the glyph puzzle on the wall near the start of this trap-filled path.

Solving the glyph puzzle doesn't deactivate the traps, but it does cause them to move, giving you a chance at slipping past them. Time your movements carefully, jumping and sprinting to get past the spinning blades and spikes.

Dash across the rickety bridge, then switch to Sallah and dig up a bucket of LEGO bits from the sparkling soil here. Smash the bucket to free the bits, then stack them to add some handrails to the trap-laden wall.

Wall of Dangers

Jump to grab the nearest handrail and wait there for the nearby spinning blade to move downward. Jump over the spinning blade when it's at its lowest point and grab the high handrail beyond. Wait for the spikes below to retract into the wall, then drop to grab the lower handrail.

Wait on the lower handrail until the next set of spikes retracts, then leap over the second spinning blade and grab the final handrail. You're home free now—jump to the nearby ledge and take a moment to catch your breath!

Free Play Goodies

Artifact Piece 3

Send a tiny character crawling through the small door beyond the first stretch of traps to reach the ledge above. Pull the ledge's lever to open a secret door below.

Continued on next page

Free Play Goodies (continued)

Enter the secret chamber and move both characters onto the pressure plate. This raises the nearby cage, giving you access to an artifact piece!

🏺 Artifact Piece 4 🏺

Return to this level with a Free Play character who carries a sword. Throw the sword at the rope near the cage at the cavern's far end to cut the rope and raise the cage. Now you can enter the nook beyond to collect an artifact piece and a purple stud!

Building Bridges

Use Indy's whip to yank down the bridge beyond the trap-filled wall, then run across. Switch to Sallah and dig up a shrine object that's buried here on the next ledge, then smash the shrine to discover some jiggling bits.

Stack the jiggling bits to add a handle to the nearby bridge. Push against the handle to extend the bridge across the next chasm, then sprint across.

Opening the Door

Shove the handle of the spinner here to rotate the spinner. Notice that the spikes below slowly begin to retract. Keep turning the spinner until the spikes have fully withdrawn into the wall.

Run past the now-harmless spike trap and pick up the green object lying on the ground beyond. Carry the object over to the green notch on the wall near the spinner.

Place the object on the green notch to create a handle. Push against the handle to open the door, then hurry through to the next area.

🏺 Artifact Piece 5 🏺

This artifact piece is clearly visible in a small nook past the first bridge, but a pair of spinning blades makes it a risky prize. Wait for the front blade to sink into the ground, then quickly dash into the nook and grab the artifact piece. You can escape with a jump if you're fast, but even if you're caught by the blade, at least you've claimed a valuable reward!

Area 4: Path of the Righteous

Following in the Footsteps

Use the hanging vine to cross the first gap you encounter along this treacherous trail, then use Indy's whip at the whip point here to pull a strange block from a nearby pillar.

Leave the block on the ground for now and solve the nearby glyph puzzle on the wall. This causes a portion of wall to slide away, revealing a hidden nook.

Insert the block you pulled from the pillar into the indicated slot in the nook. Another wall slides away, granting you access to a second nook that holds a key.

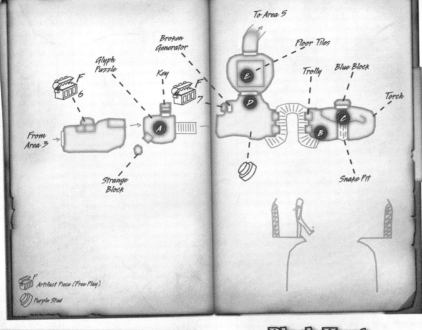

Indy can't cross the snake pit ahead, but Sallah can. Have Sallah jump the snake pit and collect a torch from the sconce on the far wall. Use the torch to light the bundle of sticks in the snake pit, clearing the way for Indy.

Use Indy's whip at the whip point above the snake pit to deactivate the spike trap, then collect the blue block. Carry the block to the left and drop from the ledge.

Take the key and insert it into the mechanism near the bridge. Turn the key to raise a fallen bridge ahead, creating a way forward. The bridge doesn't quite reach the far ledge, however. Use the handrails on the background wall to get there.

Block Hunt

Whip-swing across the next wide gap, then stack the jiggling LEGO bits on the far ledge to build a vine. Now Sallah can climb up from the lower walkway and join you.

Place the block onto the nearby trolly, then pull the lever to send it across the gap. Whip-swing across and retrieve the block on the other side.

Free Play Goodies

🔲🧍 Artifact Piece 6 🧍🔲

Toggle your Free Play character to one who's small enough to crawl through the tiny door near the start of this area. You pop out on the ledge above. Pull the lever there to raise the nearby stone steps so you may claim the artifact piece from the high ledge.

🔲🧍 Artifact Piece 7 🧍🔲

Use a character with the repair ability to fix the broken generator on the ledge beyond the bridge. This causes some handrails to pop out from the rock wall above. Jump up the handrails to reach a high, overhead ledge, where an artifact piece awaits.

Insert the block into the colorful column here to open the door. Head through to face a familiar test.

Latin Lesson

A series of floor tiles stretches out before you, each one printed with a letter. The letter "I" is flashing; jump directly onto that tile.

CAUTION

Don't jump onto an unlit floor tile! Such tiles will quickly give way, causing you to take a nasty tumble.

Another tile begins to flash after you land on the "I." This time it's an "E." Leap to that tile, and continue jumping to each tile that lights up, spelling "IEHOVAH."

Area 5: Path of the Faithful

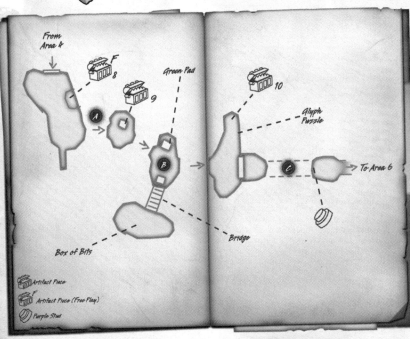

Backtrack across the bridge and place the box on the nearby green pad. Stack the jiggling bits to build a spinner, then push against the green side of the spinner's handle. Keep rotating the spinner until you open a giant door in the background.

Free Play Goodie
🚌🤖 Artifact Piece 8 🤖🚌

Return to this area with a character who has the explosion ability and blow up the silver teeth of the first ledge's lion head statue. Now you can steal the lion's snack from its mouth—a yummy artifact piece!

Gotta Have Faith

Use Indy's whip at this ledge's whip point to yank down a nearby bridge. Cross over and collect a box of LEGO bits from the far ledge.

Indy seems to have reached a dead-end: There's no obvious way across this long gap. Looks can be deceiving, however. Step out into the void to find that Indy can walk across thin air! Cross the next gap ahead in the same fashion—with a courageous leap of faith!

Leap from the Lion's Mouth

Head through the massive doorway and make one last leap of faith by running across this final gap. Indy's heart proves true, and he's able to walk cross the abyss as if there were a bridge of solid rock beneath his feet. Prepare yourself: The final test is at hand!

Artifact Piece 9

Use Indy's whip at the second ledge's whip point to tug down a massive stalactite from the ceiling. The rock smashes through a grate in the ground, enabling you to collect an artifact piece from the recess.

Artifact Piece 10

Take the torch from this area's first ledge and carry it all the way to the glyph puzzle on the fourth ledge. Light the torch near the glyph puzzle to shed extra light on its glyphs. Now you can solve the puzzle to reveal a hidden artifact piece!

Area 6: Grail Chamber

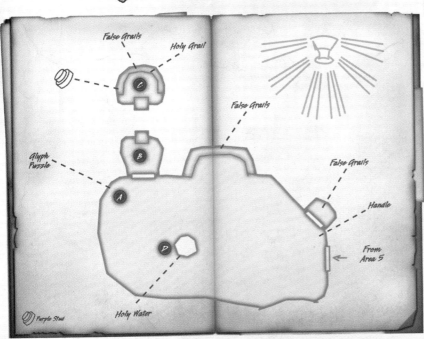

Solve the glyph puzzle to open a secret passage in the nearby wall, then dash through. Use Indy's whip to cross the gap and reach the collection of cups on the far ledge.

There's only one Holy Grail, and it's the dull-looking brown one here. Take the Holy Grail and whip-swing back across the gap.

Choose Wisely

Donovan has chosen poorly. Don't make the same mistake! Punch the enraged Grail knight until he falls to a knee, then hurry over to the glyph puzzle here.

NOTE

Ignore the handle and the cup-filled alcove to the right. You can open the alcove's cage, but all of the Grails within are false!

Dunk the Holy Grail into the pedestal filled with holy water here to pass this final test of wisdom and courage. Story complete! Sit back and enjoy the ending, Junior.

BONUS FEATURES

Spoiler alert! This chapter reveals every major secret in *LEGO Indiana Jones*, from bonus levels to super-secret characters not listed in the Characters chapter. Stop reading if you'd rather uncover these secrets yourself!!

Bonus Levels

Advance far enough through the game and you'll be able to unlock three special levels at Barnett College. First, work at completing eight artifacts by finding all 10 artifact pieces that make up each one from any eight levels of the game. Then visit the college's artifact room (up the stairs from the level select bulletin boards) to find a small diamond sitting near the middle of the room! Place the diamond on top of the central pedestal to reveal three secret passages in the floor nearby. Unfortunately, the passages are locked!

Solve all of the puzzles in Indy's office to discover a total of five treasure chests. Place each chest you find on one of the green pads in the office's center, then stack all the jiggling bits. Smash the object you build to discover a key, then take the key and return to the college's artifact room.

Opening the Levels

By the time you've managed to complete eight whole artifacts, you should also have plenty of studs. Good thing, because now you need to buy some special characters at the college's

Bazooka Trooper (Raiders)

library! You need characters with lots of different abilities to help you solve the many puzzles in Indy's office and discover a secret key that unlocks the bonus levels.

Here are the abilities you need to solve all the puzzles in Indy's office. Make sure to purchase characters who have these abilities! Flip to the Characters chapter if you need help choosing characters to buy; each one's abilities are listed there.

Insert the key into the mechanism in the middle of the artifact room, then turn it to open the three passages in the floor. Now you can visit all of the bonus levels!

 Academic ability—needed to solve the glyph puzzle on the wall of Indy's office and discover a hidden treasure chest.

 Explosion ability—needed to destroy the office's glass container to obtain a treasure chest. Also needed to destroy the big silver shields on the wall.

 Excavate ability—needed to dig up a buried treasure chest from the sparkling floor beneath the silver shields (destroy the shields first).

 Super jump ability—needed to reach the treasure chest on the office's high shelf.

 Thuggee chant ability—needed to activate the office's Kali statue to reveal a tiny door.

 Tiny size ability—needed to crawl through the tiny door and reach a treasure chest on an even higher shelf.

Bonus Level 1: Young Indy

This bonus level featuring Young Indy is a short run through *The Last Crusade's* memorable prologue. You control Young Indy himself, along with one of his Boy Scout pals. Steal the golden cross from the thieves, then make your escape by train! There are no artifact pieces or parcels to find in this level, and there's no True Adventurer bar to fill with studs. It's just a neat little extra fun that shows how Indy became so handy with a whip—and so fearful of snakes! You do unlock a couple of new Story mode characters after beating the level, though (Young Indy and Boy Scout), along with a third character you can purchase at the library (fedora). So check it out!

Bonus Level 2: Ancient City

Ancient City is a giant playground full of stuff to smash and destroy. Your goal is to collect 1,000,000 studs as fast as you can. The clock's ticking, but there's no real time limit—you're only racing against yourself to see how fast you can collect those studs. Gain an edge by unlocking lots of characters with an array of special abilities. Pick a bazooka trooper as your main character, as they're a bit quicker at blowing stuff up compared to enemy officers. Interact with everything you see and search for hidden doorways to tiny rooms filled with studs. Don't waste time tracking down tools, such as wrenches—instead, toggle your character to one that has the special abilities you need. Above all, have fun!

Bonus Level 3: Warehouse

Like Ancient City, your goal in Warehouse is to earn 1,000,000 studs as fast as possible. The setup is much different, though: Rather than giving you lots of stuff to destroy, you're  presented with a host of blocks to carry and place onto green pads found all over the floor. Once placed, each block becomes a portion of track with a spinner in the middle. (Look at the symbol on the blocks to see what type of track they'll create when placed—a turn or a straight.) After placing a block, you can use it's spinner to rotate the track however you like. This lets you build your own racecourse through the warehouse!

 There are several vehicles in the warehouse, including an awesome tank that can roll over just about anything. While most vehicles are painfully slow here, there is a fast one: Use a bazooka to blast apart the hanging crates to the left and discover a super-fast motorcycle! There's no faster way to cruise the warehouse than with this bad boy.

 Building a track and racing along it is pretty neat, but it's also time consuming and not very profitable. If you're just looking to earn studs fast, fire at the bull's-eye target to the right. The target never blows up; it just pumps out studs each time it's hit. Use a character with a bazooka, machine gun, pistol, or some other firearm, and keep shooting the target until you hit the 1,000,000 mark. Cha-ching!

Secret Characters

Han Solo

Han Solo is a super-secret playable character in *LEGO Indiana Jones*, and unlocking him takes some effort. First, you must find five *Star Wars* characters that are cleverly hidden within five levels. Most of these can only be discovered during Free Play mode, and we intentionally left them out of the walkthrough to avoid spoiling the surprise. But this is the Bonus Features section, so we'd better reveal them!

The Lost Temple: C-3PO

Replay the Lost Temple level in Free Play and use a character with the explosion ability to blast through the silver bars at the far-right side of the Idol Chamber area. This grants you access to a secret area, where you not only find a hidden artifact piece, but also an odd drum with C-3PO's head sitting on top! Bash the drum to free the protocol droid's entrapped body. Four more *Star Wars* characters to find!

Into the Mountains: Luke Skywalker

Luke's gotten himself stuck in the Mountain Pass area of the Into the Mountains level. Drop into the icy ravine near the exit point and use a character with the explosion ability to free young Skywalker from his predicament—before some monster comes along and eats him!

City of Danger: Chewbacca

While exploring this level's final area in Free Play mode, use a character with the academic ability to solve the glyph puzzle near the truck depot. You're then able to enter a familiar cantina, where the level's parcel is found. There's another treat to find in here, though: Use a tiny-size character to crawl through the little door in the cantina and pay a visit to Chewbacca, who sits in a private booth.

Free the Slaves: Princess Leia

Like the slave children, Leia is being held prisoner in the Slave Pen area of the Free the Slaves level. Run to the foreground and drop to the lower ledge, then destroy the silver rubble with a character who has the explosion ability. Fool the guard at the window with an enemy disguise character to gain entry to the prison cell beyond, where Leia awaits rescue. The prison looks oddly out of place, yet strangely familiar....

Desert Ambush: R2-D2

R2-D2 is the only *Star Wars* character that can be found during regular Story mode. In the Desert Ambush level's very first area, have Indy ride a horse over to the left ledges, then leap from the saddle to reach the high cliff above. This is how you obtain one of the level's artifact pieces, but also notice the whip point up here. Use Indy's whip there to pull R2-D2 down from above!

Unlocking Han

After finding all five of Han's buddies, visit Barnett College's library to find Han Solo available for purchase. As you might expect, Han carries a blaster pistol that's quite powerful. He also throws his fists even faster than Indy! Han doesn't have any special gameplay abilities, though…other than being extremely cool, of course.

NOTE

Into the Mountains is the only level in which Santa Clause will appear.

Santa Clause

This jolly old elf is much easier to get a hold of compared to Han. Simply visit the college's mail room and spend a few studs to purchase the "Secret Characters" parcel, which is unlocked right from the start of the game. After doing so, pause the game and turn on the Secret Characters option, which now appears under the pause menu's Extras settings. Then choose to revisit the Into the Mountains level from *Raiders* in Free Play mode to find St. Nick among your Free Play crew!

Dancing Girl 2

By purchasing the "Secret Characters" parcel to unlock Santa Clause, you also unlock this lovely dancing girl. Follow the steps outlined above, then choose to Free Play the Shanghai Showdown level from *The Temple of Doom*. Cycle through your Free Play characters to discover a beautiful new female character!

NOTE

Shanghai Showdown is the only level in which Dancing Girl 2 will appear.

Appendices

Parcels

Find a parcel in each level of the game and mail it in a postbox to send it back to Barnett College. Then visit the college's mail room to purchase the parcels you've found. The following table details each parcel in the game.

PARCELS

Name	How to Unlock	Cost	Effect
Secret Characters	Unlocked from the start	25,000	Unlocks "Santa" and "Dancing Girl 2" for use in Free Play.
Fertilizer	Unlocked from the start	7,500	All animals have the ability to poo (press the Use button while riding).
Disguises	Unlocked from the start	12,500	Gives all characters funny disguises.
Silhouettes	Unlocked from the start	10,000	Turns all character/enemy/creature models into shadowy silhouettes.
Beep Beep	Unlocked from the start	7,500	Vehicle horns can be honked (press the Use button while driving).

PARCELS (CONTINUED)

Ice Rink	Unlocked from the start	15,000	Makes you slide about as if the ground were made of ice.
Fast Fix	Find and mail the "The Lost Temple" level's parcel	30,000	Lets you repair broken machinery with a wrench much faster.
Super Slap	Find and mail the "Into the Mountains" level's parcel	25,000	Melee attacks do much greater damage.
Treasure x2	Find and mail the "City of Danger" level's parcel	1,000,000	Doubles the value of each stud you collect.
Fast Dig	Find and mail "The Well of Souls" level's parcel	50,000	Lets you dig up buried objects with a shovel much faster.
Fast Build	Find and mail the "Pursuing the Ark" level's parcel	40,000	Lets you stack jiggling LEGO bits much faster than normal.
Artifact Detector	Find and mail the "Opening the Ark" level's parcel	250,000	Makes onscreen arrows appear, which point toward each level's hidden artifact pieces.
Treasure x4	Find and mail the "Shanghai Showdown" level's parcel	2,000,000	Quadruples the value of each stud you collect.
Poo Treasure	Find and mail the "Pankot Secrets" level's parcel	70,000	Animals can be made to poo out studs (press the Use button while riding).
Super Scream	Find and mail the "Temple of Kali" level's parcel	80,000	Makes Willie's scream knock enemies away and defeat them.
Character Treasure	Find and mail the "Free the Slaves" level's parcel	100,000	Enemies yield studs when they're broken apart (defeated).
Treasure x6	Find and mail the "Escape the Mines" level's parcel	3,000,000	Causes each stud you collect to be worth 6 times its normal value.
Regenerate Hearts	Find and mail the "Battle on the Bridge" level's parcel	150,000	Causes you to quickly regenerate lost hearts over time.
Parcel Detector	Find and mail "The Hunt for Sir Richard" level's parcel	125,000	Makes onscreen arrows appear, which point toward each level's hidden parcel.
Disarm Enemies	Find and mail the "Castle Rescue" level's parcel	100,000	Enemies will still carry guns but are unable to fire.
Name	**How to Unlock**	**Cost**	**Effect**
Treasure x8	Find and mail the "Motorcycle Escape" level's parcel	4,000,000	Causes each stud you collect to be worth 8 times its normal value.
Treasure Magnet	Find and mail the "Trouble in the Sky" level's parcel	100,000	Draws loose studs toward you.
Treasure x10	Find and mail the "Desert Ambush" level's parcel	5,000,000	Causes each stud you collect to be worth 10 times its normal value.
Invincibility	Find and mail the "Temple of the Grail" level's parcel	1,000,000	Makes you impervious to damage from attacks.

Achievements

For your convenience, here's the complete list of every gameplay achievement in *LEGO Indiana Jones*. You'll meet most of these simply by playing through the adventure, but a few require a bit more effort. Satisfy all of these achievements and consider yourself a truly awesome adventurer!

ACHIEVEMENTS

Achievement	Description	Points
There is nothing to fear here.	Complete "The Lost Temple" level in Story mode.	10
It's important, Marion...trust me.	Complete the "Into The Mountains" level in Story mode.	10
Belloq's staff is too long.	Complete the "City of Danger" level in Story mode.	10

ACHIEVEMENTS (CONTINUED)

Why did it have to be snakes?	Complete the "The Well of Souls" level in Story mode.	10
I'm making this up as I go along.	Complete the "Pursing the Ark" level in Story mode.	10
Keep your eyes shut!	Complete the "Opening the Ark" level in Story mode.	10
Short Round, step on it!	Complete the "Shanghai Showdown" level in Story mode.	10
I had bugs for lunch.	Complete the "Pankot Secrets" level in Story mode.	10
Quit fooling around.	Complete the "Free The Slaves" level in Story mode.	10
Take the left tunnel!	Complete the "Escape the Mines" level in Story mode.	10
Prepare to meet Kali.	Complete the "Battle on the Bridge" level in Story mode.	10
X marks the spot.	Complete "The Hunt for Sir Richard" level in Story mode.	10
DON'T call me Junior!	Complete the "Castle Rescue" level in Story mode.	10
We're not going in the boat?	Complete the "Motorcycle Escape" level in Story mode.	10
No ticket.	Complete the "Trouble in the Sky" level in Story mode.	10
They're well out of range, Dad.	Complete the "Desert Ambush" level in Story mode.	10
He chose...poorly.	Complete the "Temple of the Grail" level in Story mode.	10
That belongs in a museum.	Complete the "Young Indy" level in Story mode.	10
This...this is history.	Collect all artifacts.	40
Your mail is on your desk.	Post all parcels.	40
Fortune and glory, kid.	Complete the game to 100%.	100
Shoot them. Shoot them both.	Find and use all of the different weapons in the game.	25
You chose...wisely.	Unlock all of the available characters.	35
You will become a true believer.	Use a Thuggee statue 50 times.	15
Bad dates.	Give 50 bananas to monkeys.	15
What a cautious fellow I am.	Destroy 50 objects with a bazooka or other explosive device.	15
You call this archaeology?	Use a scholar character's academic ability 50 times.	15
The best digger in Cairo.	Uncover 50 pieces of buried treasure using the excavation ability.	15
The trouble with her is the noise.	Shatter 50 glass objects using Willie's scream ability.	15
Start the engines, Jock!	Use a mechanic character's repair ability 50 times.	15
How we say good-bye in Germany.	Access restricted enemy locations 50 times.	15
Show a little backbone, will ya?	Destroy 100 snakes.	15
Maybe I tread on fortune cookies.	Destroy 100 scarabs.	15
I hate these guys.	Destroy 200 enemy guards or thuggee.	15
Oh, rats!	Destroy 100 rats.	15
We go for a ride.	Perform 250 whip swings in the game.	15
Throw me the idol.	Perform 150 whip grabs in the game.	15
I can't believe what you did!	Disarm 100 enemies with the whip.	15
He no nuts. He's crazy.	Smash 250 LEGO objects.	20
A source of unspeakable power.	Build 250 LEGO objects.	20
It's not the years, honey...	Complete any level without dying.	40
Indy! Cover your heart!	Complete any level without losing hearts or studs.	50
That's for blasphemy.	Destroy Indy with Henry Jones.	20
Nice try, Lao Che.	Destroy Lao Che with Indy.	20
Good-bye, Dr Jones.	Destroy Indy with Lao Che.	20
Adios, Satipo.	Be destroyed by a trap while playing as Satipo.	20
You cheat very big!	Unlock all cheats.	30

ACHIEVEMENTS (CONTINUED)

Achievement	Description	Points
Got lost in his own museum.	Unlock secret area in the museum.	30
Hey! You call him Dr. Jones!	Create and name a custom build character.	10
No time for love, Dr Jones.	Complete story mode in under 2 hours.	75
Total		1,000

Chasing the Ark

Fighting

CONCEPT ART

Marion's Cafe
—Nepal

Kalis Temple —29/10/07
colour sketch

RESCUE THE SH...
MINING...
SI...

Barnett College

Jungle
—India

Shanghai
Streets

REAR VIEW OF TEMPLE -
VIEWING PLATFORM

Cairo Streets

Sir Richard's Tomb

Ark Room

The Well of Souls